MW00612206

IPOS, SPACS, & DIRECT LISTINGS

WHAT ARE THEY?

SHOULD I INVEST?

Nam Viet Nguyen

ISBN: 978-1-7371834-1-9 (Paperback)
978-1-7371834-2-6 (Hardcover)
978-1-7371834-0-2 (eBook)

Library of Congress Control Number: 2021938711

All content reflects our opinion at a given time and can change as time progresses. All information should be taken as an opinion and should not be misconstrued for professional or legal advice. The contents of this book are informational in nature and are not legal or tax advice, and the authors and publishers are not engaged in the provision of legal, tax, or any other advice.

Front cover image by 100Covers
Book Design by FormattedBooks

Printed by Nam Viet Nguyen in the United States of America.

First printing edition 2021.

www.namvietnguyen.com

DEDICATION

For my wife Tram, who supports my various endeavors with words of encouragement.

For my son Remy, for whom I want to provide a better life just like my parents did for me.

For my parents Hong and Mai, a special dedication in their native tongue:

Tôi muốn cảm ơn ba mẹ tôi, người đã rời bỏ quê hương và hy sinh tất cả để đem lại cho tôi một tương lai tươi sáng.

ACKNOWLEDGMENT

Thank you to M.K. Williams, who coached and guided me throughout the writing and publishing process.

Thank you to Nhan Le, Spencer Yoon, Allen Pham, Raymond Dipasupil, David Nguyen, Albert Martinez, and Jose Elamparo for sharing their valuable inputs.

Thank you to Sara Bruya for her editorial input.

CONTENTS

CHAPTER 1

Introduction

Over the years, I would get countless text messages asking me, "Should I invest in this IPO?". Friends, family, and colleagues would reach out and ask for my thoughts on the latest hot IPOs and I would spend hours trying to explain how it works and why they should invest or not. I would write long emails or text messages, spend hours on the phone, forward finance articles, and do simple valuation calculations on napkins at happy hour.

Enthusiastic about all the questions and being afraid I might have missed an important detail in these conversations, I tried in earnest to find a book for my friends to read so they could get a feel for what IPOs are and how to go about investing. I found that most finance books are inaccessible, often requiring a finance or business undergraduate degree to understand the dense finance jargon. The books I found were full of theories and outdated examples of companies that aren't relevant today. I realized most people don't need a rundown of the efficient market theory or a hundred years of economic history.

Most people just wanted to know two things:

1. What is an IPO and how does it work?
2. Should I invest in the IPO?

I wrote this book to answer those two questions for all my friends and family that have asked and for anyone that might have posed that question before.

I try to keep it simple. The book starts by explaining the various ways a company can go public and then I share my research framework to determine whether it is a good investment or not. If we determine it's a good investment, I'll try to convince you to hold it for the long term. I wanted to use fun and contemporary examples of companies we buy from and interact with every day. I wanted to have memorable illustrations that brought my ideas to life. This is a book for those who choose to be active, want to learn about individual companies, and buy individual stocks with the goal of earning great returns over the long term. Overall, I wanted to share everything I had learned about IPOs and stocks in a short and enjoyable read. When the Covid-19 pandemic shut everything down, I finally found the time and energy to put pen to paper and write the book I would be proud to share with aspiring investors.

I hope this book empowers you.

PART 1

HOW DOES A COMPANY GO PUBLIC?

CHAPTER 2

Initial Public Offering (IPO)

What is an Initial Public Offering (commonly referred to by its acronym "IPO")? Let's start with the basics and define what an IPO is and ponder why a company would even want to take their business public to trade on a stock exchange. We'll then walk through the process of how they do that exactly.

Why Go Public at All?

In an Initial Public Offering, a company for the first time offers its equity shares (ownership in the company) to the public. They will choose an exchange such as the New York Stock Exchange (NYSE) or the Nasdaq and those shares will trade publicly, allowing anyone with a brokerage account to buy and sell the shares.

Let's use an example of a start-up to walk through what it takes to reach the IPO stage. This start-up has been around for a few years and has had various venture capital investments (these are made by rich investors in the early days before any profit is made by the company, providing a leap of faith investment) and years of steady revenue growth. The IPO represents the first time public investors will have an opportunity to invest in the company. Retail investors, like you and me, along with mutual funds and hedge funds who are known as institutional investors, will be able to own shares in the newly public company.

The IPO will allow the company to sell a portion of itself—let's use an example of 10%—to raise additional capital. Let's say the company is going public at a $10 billion valuation, so 10% of equity up for sale means they are attempting to raise $1 billion by selling that amount of stock. The $1 billion they raise by selling stock will go into their cash line item on the balance sheet and be ready to use for expanding and growing the business.

There are many reasons for a company to transition from a private company into a public one. The largest driver is the need for more capital to grow. Simply put, they want more cash on their balance sheet to implement growth initiatives and will sell ownership in the company (equity) to fund it. Examples of growth initiatives could be opening a second factory to manufacture, building a new branch or headquarters, launching a new product line, etc. The company will have exhausted a long list of venture capital rounds (private shares sold to venture capitalists to raise money while the company is still young) and believes it is ready and mature enough to withstand the rigors of a public market, which requires quarterly earnings reports and various disclosures. An IPO will also allow venture capitalists who invested in the company early to sell their shares and exit, hopefully reaping gains. It will also allow the founders and employees a chance to sell their stock so they can also reap the rewards from their early commitment to the company.

Employees of a start-up often look forward to selling their shares so they can buy homes, cars, pay for school, etc. Employees selling stock should not be seen as a lack of belief in the company's prospects; it's more likely that they sacrificed higher pay in the start-up phase for those early equity shares. Those shares were granted early on in place of a higher salary to incentivize employees to work hard and potentially enjoy large gains the company goes public. For founders and employees, there is usually a lock-up period that prevents these holders from selling within the first six months of the initial public offering, to prevent a torrent of selling that can depress share price performance.

As I mentioned earlier in this chapter, the company's employees have been granted shares and this is the first time they can sell them. All company employees must hold onto the shares for around six months or more after the IPO before the lock-up period expires, and they can freely sell. This is implemented so they can avoid a big block of the company stock being sold all at once which could cause the price to be depressed or crash.

Hiring an Investment Bank

Here is a flow chart to summarize all of the steps involved in an IPO.

Exhibit 1 – The Initial Public Offering (IPO) Process

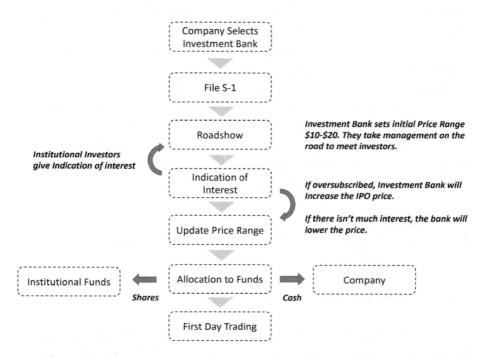

In addition to raising money, an IPO can allow some early investors to sell their shares to the public at the same time as well. To make it simple, let's assume no early investors sell. In this case, the entire $1 billion raised will go into the company's balance sheet as cash. When starting to explore a possible IPO, the company will usually hire an investment bank to help gauge interest and market the shares to potential investors.

Think of investment banks as salespeople and the product they are selling are companies. More specifically, they are selling fractional ownership of companies. Similar to real estate agents or car salesmen, they know a lot about their products and are considered experts in various companies across numerous industries. Similar to cars and real estate, no two businesses are exactly the same and have different qualities that will determine their price. Ultimately, the job of an investment bank is to generate interest in the company they are selling.

The investment bank analyzes the financial statements and prospects of the company and builds a presentation to help explain why the company is a great investment to potential institutional investors, including mutual funds, pension funds, and hedge funds. The investment bank also puts together the S-1 initial registration form or simply "S-1" for short. This is often also referred to as the prospectus. This document will cover financial statements, plans for the capital raised, risks, the definition of terms, an overview of the management team, market dynamics, competitors, and ultimately why this company is a great asset to own. Remember, the investment bank is marketing and selling this company, so it is in their best interest (and their client's best interest) to present the company in the best light possible.

Chapter 8 and beyond will be dedicated to navigating, understanding, and analyzing what is reported in the S-1 so we can answer the question: Should we invest in this company?

Going on a Roadshow

Investment banks only market to institutional investors such as pension funds and mutual funds because these funds collectively manage billions of dollars and have the ability to invest and buy millions of shares. The marketing process would be burdensome if management were instead to meet with millions of retail investors who can only buy a few shares at a time.

These important institutional investors get to meet the management team face to face when the investment bank flies the company's management team on a multi-city trip called a "roadshow" to meet these powerful potential investors in financial centers including New York, San Francisco, Boston, Los Angeles, London, and Hong Kong. The investment bank's efforts are focused on garnering interest and leveraging their connections to create demand for these IPO shares. The investment banks are looking for investors who will buy these shares with the intent of holding for the long term. While the roadshow allows for the company to tell its story, it also allows institutional investors to present themselves as long-term investors that are worthy of being allocated more shares than their competitors.

After the roadshow is completed, the investment banks start making calls to see who is interested in buying the stock, and funds can call in to "indicate their interest" by putting down how many shares they want. If the banks do their jobs well, the interest for the shares will be greater than the shares available. This creates a situation where the IPO demand is greater than the supply. For example, let's suppose $2 billion of shares are requested for $1 billion in shares available in the IPO. This means the IPO is oversubscribed two times over or 2x oversubscribed.

A successful IPO is one that garners a lot of demand and provides a nice opening day increase for its investors—known as the IPO "pop".

Dividing Up the Pie (IPO Allocation)

After various institutional investors conduct their due diligence by reading the S-1, attending the roadshow, and building their own financial model of the company, they decide if they want to buy the shares or not. If they want to participate in the IPO, they submit an "Indication of interest" to the investment bank by stating how much they would like to invest. Due to the dynamic nature of the IPO price, which is often given as a range and not a set share price, funds express their interest in total monetary amounts. For example, "We would like to indicate interest for a total of $1,000,000." After the banks decide the final share price, they then debate how many shares are allocated to which funds. They wait until the day of the IPO to inform the funds of the exact number of shares that have been allocated. For popular IPOs, with lots of interest from various funds, the allocation process can continue well into the night before the IPO.

The various banks involved in the deal work together to decide which investors get how many shares in a process known as allocation. The bigger clients will demand more and often receive more. This is purposely done to reward the clients for doing business with the banks, including participating in other deals and trading with the firm, another source of revenue for the bank. If your management firm does not have a strong relationship with the investment bank, you can forget about getting any significant amount of shares. Often, an indication of interest for $1 million worth of shares will result in an allocation of $50,000 or $100,000 for the smaller funds that don't have a strong history with the investment banks.

The table below demonstrates a fictional pecking order: long term focused funds such as pension funds and sovereign wealth funds will get large allocations while smaller hedge funds and high frequency trading firms will get small allocations because they are more likely to sell those shares after the "pop" on the first day. For mutual funds, it depends.

The investment banks look at the fund's holdings to see if they own similar companies and are long term investors to see if they are a good match, rewarding the funds that are more likely to keep the shares as a long-term investment. For a hot IPO, often no one gets their full indication. After the allocation process is completed, the bank will inform the fund of its allocation. The funds will receive their new shares on the morning of the IPO. Here is a sample of what the indication/allocation table looks like before the first day of trading.

Table 1 – Indication and Allocation

Asset Manager	Indication of Interest	Actual Allocation
State Pension Fund	$20,000,000	$3,000,000
Sovereign Wealth Fund	$10,000,000	$2,000,000
Large Mutual Fund	$5,000,000	$1,000,000
Small Mutual Fund	$2,000,000	$750,000
Hedge Fund	$1,000,000	$250,000
Proprietary Trading Firm	$1,000,000	$0

The First Day of Trading

Usually, the company and its management team are invited to the stock exchange (NYSE or Nasdaq) to ring the opening bell that day and are invited to sit down for an interview on CNBC and Bloomberg News, two finance-orientated news channels. If successful, the first day price will have a "pop", which is an increase of 10%, or 25%, or 50%, creating instant profits for those that invested in the IPO and creating wealth for employees and early investors who own shares of the company. This IPO "pop" is shown often in the headline across news outlets and is often indicative of a successful IPO in the minds of the public.

A Broken IPO

We walked through an ideal example of an IPO, where shares are oversubscribed because funds are fighting to get their allocation. On the other side, there are IPOs that have lackluster demand and on the first day of trading actually fall below their IPO price. This is called a "broken IPO" because the price went below its IPO offered price creating an immediate loss for funds that were allocated shares. An example of a recent broken IPO is King.com, the mobile video game maker of Candy Crush Saga, which went public on March 24, 2014 at $22.50 and closed the day at $19 per share, losing nearly 10% in its first day of trading. There was lackluster demand for the stock at that price given how poor the performance of its mobile gaming peer Zynga had been for a few years since its IPO. A broken IPO can have a lingering psychological effect as well, as the first day can leave a bad impression and perpetuate more selling of the stock as investors seek to exit quickly to limit any further losses.

Exhibit 2 - Successful IPO vs Broken IPO

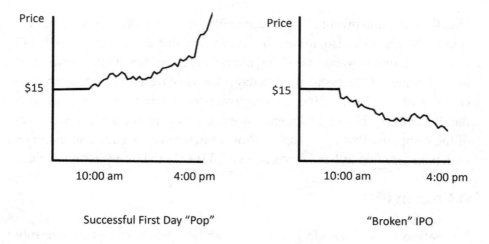

Successful First Day "Pop"   "Broken" IPO

The "Greenshoe" or Overallotment Option

The overallotment option, known as the "Greenshoe option", allows for the investment bank to buy an additional amount of shares of the company, usually up to 15% of the shares offered. The investment bank wants to make sure prices are stable on the first day of trading because a weak performance can reflect negatively on both the company and the investment bank. In an ideal world, the process is a success with shares experiencing the "pop" on the first day and is up anywhere from 10–50% or even higher. In the scenario where the IPO price falls below the offer price on the first day of trading (known as "breaking issue" or a "broken IPO"), the investment bank can exercise their Greenshoe option and buy back shares at or below the offering price, creating demand and an upward movement in price. The investment bank initially oversells the IPO offering by 15% and can buy back that 15% in the public market. This very act of buying in the public market stabilizes the price amidst a price drop.

Why is the overallotment option called "Greenshoe" anyways? It was first implemented for the Green Shoe Manufacturing Company in 1919, now commonly known as the shoe retailer Stride Rite.

Leaving Money on the Table

A big first day gain via the "pop" is the common indicator of a successful IPO as investors, founders, employees, and early investors including venture capital funds see a large immediate gain. Technically, it means the investment bank underpriced the company shares and its true value is actually what it starts trading at on the first day (the opening price). In our example, the company's IPO raised $1 billion by offering up shares at $25 per share. In total, they are selling 40,000,000 shares at $25 per share, for a total initial public offering capital raise of $1,000,000,000. On the day of the IPO, the first day of trading, let's say the company's shares pop and close at $30 per share for a one-day gain of 20%. Everyone who were allocated shares are happy because they were able to capitalize on a quick gain of 20% in one day. The investment bankers earn their fees and generate goodwill with the funds they've allocated shares to, deepening personal relationships for future business. However, the company could've priced their shares at $30 per share and reaped an additional $5 per share or an additional $200,000,000 of capital. They left that money on the table because they underpriced their shares relative to the market value on that first day.

Even with full knowledge of that pricing error, no company or investment bank wants to see an IPO with a first day gain of 0%. That's true despite "no money left on the table" being the rational goal to strive for. It would lack the excitement and media coverage and would not reward the institutional investors that put in a big order. Worst, a flat first day can trigger selling and drive the stock price down. Bankers and companies are willing to lose out on pricing shares higher in order to ensure a big and exciting first trading day "pop". That first day "pop" creates strong momentum for the stock going forward so investment banks often try to find the perfect price that raises capital for the company while also leaving some money on the table.

What is the perfect IPO price? It's more art than science, but the banks price the shares initially within a range, say $20–$30, and ask their clients what they think the stock is worth. The clients are investment funds that use teams of equity research analysts and portfolio managers to dissect financial statements and build their own valuation models to formulate an opinion of the company. The funds share that price with the banks and vice versa. The investment banks collect a handful of the fund's opinions and compare everyone's view of that price to build consensus on a final price. Based on order sizes and conversations they adjust that price to create more demand than can be met by the shares offered. This creates an environment where firms are likely to buy on the first day because they didn't get as many shares as they wanted and they view the shares as undervalued, thus creating a bidding up environment that leads to that coveted initial trading day "pop". Akin to the Goldilocks story, they try to price it so it's not too hot or too cold, somewhere in the middle ("just right") that makes everyone happy.

Investment Banking

So that's what investment bankers do!

Yes, you might have heard about investment banking and the allure it holds for finance majors and business school graduates but always wondered exactly what is it that they actually do? They help companies and governments raise money. They help companies raise money by selling stocks (equity ownership in the company) or by selling bonds (effectively a loan to the company that is paid back). With governments, including at the Federal level (the Treasury) and local level (toll roads, libraries, subway systems), investment banks help sell bonds to fund new projects. Governments pay back these bonds through tax revenue. Investment banks charge a percentage of the capital they help raise, called the underwriting fee. The fee is usually between 5–15% of the total amount and on average is 7%. Governments can't issue stock because you can't be owners of the Government.

One other thing investment bankers are tasked with is advising on mergers, acquisitions, and spin-offs. If Company A wants to buy company B, they hire an investment bank to analyze the potential deal and give their opinion on how much should be paid, how much company A would save in cost synergies (these are savings in operating costs when companies merge, such as from eliminating jobs that overlap), and if the deal would likely be approved by regulatory bodies.

Investment bankers and real estate agents operate in much the same way and leverage the same skill sets. Let's look at the similarities:

1. **Unique Asset** - Both sell unique and expensive assets as no two companies or homes are the same.

2. **Peer Comparable** - To price companies, bankers also use peer comparables to get metrics like Price to Earnings. Agents use Price Per Square Footage and look at prices of comparable homes such as all the 3-bedroom, 2-bath homes that have been sold in the area. Also, both care about recent prices; it doesn't matter what the company/ house sold for 10 years ago. What matters is what price can you get today. They will know what a good price to bid is and will tell you if you are underbidding or overbidding. We'll explore this some more in the valuation chapter.

3. **Know the Neighborhood** - A good agent knows the area well: schools, cafes, and restaurants within walking distance, grocery stores, busy streets, crime rate, freeway access, and traffic, etc. A good banker knows the industry well too: profit margins, revenue growth, up and coming competitors, regulatory challenges, etc.

4. **Commissions/Fees** - Both work for commissions/fees. Real Estate agents take 6% of the total value of the house (split half between the buying and selling agent so each gets 3%). The investment banking syndicate (fancy word for a group of banks split a roughly 7% underwriting fee on the capital raised for the company. Unlike real estate, this relationship is uneven with the bulge bracket banks earning more and the smaller banks earning less.

5. **Access is Key** - The best agents know when a desirable house is going to be listed and will alert their customers to move fast. The best bankers will have access to the hottest IPOs and be able to allocate them to their clients.

Ta da! You now know what investment bankers do.

Exhibit 3 - Investment Bankers and Real Estate Agents

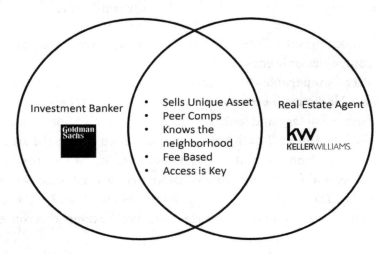

Retail Investors Have to Wait

The IPO process is centered around distributing shares to large institutional investors including the likes of mutual, pension, and hedge funds. These funds have the capital to buy a large number of shares and usually hold for the long term. From the perspective of the investment bank and company management team, it is desirable to have large institutional shareholders as a signal to the whole market that sophisticated investors are backing you. On the roadshow, banks focus on introducing the management team to institutional investors because they manage billions in assets and are represented by a few portfolio managers that invest on behalf of pension retirement plans and sovereign wealth funds that total hundreds of billions of dollars. This is not a process where anyone with a brokerage account can come and meet the company. It's easier to win over a few major funds that manage billions instead of focusing on thousands of individuals with much less in their retail brokerage accounts. For regular Joes like you and me, also known as retail investors, we won't be able to access the shares at the IPO price, but we can buy shares on the first day when it starts trading. Unfortunately, this is often the only option for retail investors to be able to access these shares for the first time. With that said, in our example, retail investors won't be able to get shares at $25 but can buy them on the first day for $30. Yes, we'll have missed out on the first day's gains, but we'll get to participate in all the gains thereafter. In the long term, this price difference is minimal if we identify the companies that have great long term growth prospects. So, while we might miss the first day "pop", we'll be able to participate in the stock's gain every day afterward.

Private to Public Transition

The transition from a private to a public company invites a lot of new challenges for everyone in the company, so having a large set of long term oriented institutional investors is in their best interest. As a public company, there are a host of regulatory requirements that shine a spotlight on the company. Each quarter, the company will have to report its financial results and key metrics to the public. Shares are volatile around these earnings reports and Wall Street has a keen habit of punishing stocks that do not meet their short-term expectations of revenue and earnings growth. As a private company, struggling for a few quarters is expected as start-ups learn to operate, invest, and position themselves for long term growth with the inevitable bumps along the road. Public companies, facing quarterly scrutiny from investors and Wall Street sell-side analysts, might be incentivized to focus on short term financial goals instead of long-term investments that lead to sustainable competitive advantage. As a public stock, the shares are judged daily by investors, analysts, and media outlets even if no significant news or development arises.

Let's summarize the pros and cons of going public using the traditional IPO route for the company.

Table 2 - Pros vs Cons of the Traditional IPO Route

Pros	Cons
Guidance from experienced Investment Banks	Inefficient pricing by investment bankers leads to money being left on the table
Shares allocated to institutional investors who will hold for the long term	Shares allocated to a small group of institutional investors/ funds; retail investors miss out
Raise capital needed for growth	High Investment Banking fees of ~ 7% of capital raised
Create awareness through splashy headlines	Roadshow takes management's time away from running the company
Lock-up period prevents a wave of selling	
Greenshoe option to stabilize the price	

Just how many IPOs are there to analyze each year anyways?

A lot.

Exhibit 4 – Annual IPO Listings (1999 – 2020)

Annual IPO Listings

Source: FactSet

Here is a look at how many IPOs are conducted each year. IPO activity is typically weaker around recessions, including from 2001-2003 and from 2008-2009. Coming out of a recession, they bounce back and maintain that strength for several years until falling off a cliff in the next recession. Recent IPO activity has been surprisingly strong as 2020 broke the previous record set during the Dot-Com bubble of the 1999s.

In summary, an IPO is a traditional process where an investment bank guides a private company to sell its shares in the public market for the first time. These are the basics for what I consider a "traditional" IPO, but there are several alternatives. We'll look at those next to understand why companies might prefer the alternative path.

CHAPTER 3

Special Purpose Acquisition Company (SPAC)

In the next few chapters, we will explore alternatives to the traditional IPO path discussed in Chapter 2. These different paths to the public markets may be a better option for private companies for a variety of reasons, the two largest of which are time and money.

Alternatives to the Traditional IPO

Companies have more options than ever to "go public" outside of the traditional IPO route, which tends to be expensive because the investment banks they hire take a big chunk of the total capital raised. Seven percent is a sizable amount. For example, a $100 million IPO leaves the company with only an additional $93 million in their coffers, with $7 million going to the investment banks. You can see why alternatives would be very appealing.

Special Purpose Acquisition Company (SPAC)

One alternative to the traditional IPO is for a private company to merge with a Special Purpose Acquisition Company, commonly called a "SPAC". SPACs are considered "blank check companies" or "shell companies" because they have no business operations of their own. They raise money for the sole purpose of trying to acquire a private company using that cash, effectively bringing that private company into the public market through a merger.

Let's walk through the process. A SPAC is formed and offers a unit at its IPO. A unit is offered for $10, which usually includes 1 share and 1 warrant to buy future shares. After the IPO, shares and warrants are traded separately. The cash raised in an IPO goes into a trust, where it earns interest until a target company is acquired. The interest earned is minimal compared to a money market fund or a savings account. After a deal for an acquisition is announced, if investors don't like the deal, they can redeem their common stock for a share of the cash in the trust. This allows shareholders to reject the deal and get their cash back while providing an option to participate in that deal at the $10 share price. This is possible because while the deal is announced, it hasn't occurred yet. Shareholders must approve of the deal and have some time to redeem the shares for $10 if they don't want a stake in the new company. Even easier, they can sell their shares in the market at market price. Theoretically, it will never go below $10 because that is the amount for which each share can be redeemed.

SPACs raise money with the intended goal of acquiring a private company down the line, effectively bringing that private company into the public markets. First, a sponsor submits an S-1 prospectus with the SEC, similar to the traditional IPO process. The SPAC raises money through an IPO, selling one unit (share and warrant) for $10. All the money raised is then put into a trust earning a small interest rate and sits there while the management team goes out and finds a private company to acquire. The IPO proceeds are held in a trust for up to a defined period of time, usually no more than two years, while the SPAC management team works on acquiring a private business, known as the "De-SPAC Transaction".

The total amount raised is important because the target acquisition company must have a fair market value of 80% or more of the SPAC's trust funds. As an example, let's say a SPAC raised $1 billion. By law, it has to acquire a company whose fair market value is 80%, or $800 million, or higher. When investors buy into the IPO, they are buying a "unit" which is just 1 share of common stock and a warrant. Warrants are worth a fraction of the stock and act like a call option, which allows you to buy stock in the future. Unlike an option, exercising that warrant will allow the company to take the proceeds onto its balance sheet. This increases total shares outstanding and dilutes shareholders, as it increases the total amount of shares available by the number of warrants exercised. For our purposes, we will keep things simple and focus on the shares of the SPAC.

Shares of the SPAC are worth $10 and absent any formal announcement of a merger, we can expect the shares to trade at $10 in theory. However, in the real world, the shares of the SPAC will trade up or down based on rumors and speculations that might appear in headlines and may or may not materialize. We will work through an example in Chapter 21 which is focused on SPAC valuation.

SPACs are an appealing alternative to the traditional IPO process and PIPEs provide additional capital so the SPAC can merge with a bigger company than originally intended. Here is a flow chart that summarizes the SPAC process.

Exhibit 5 – The SPAC Process

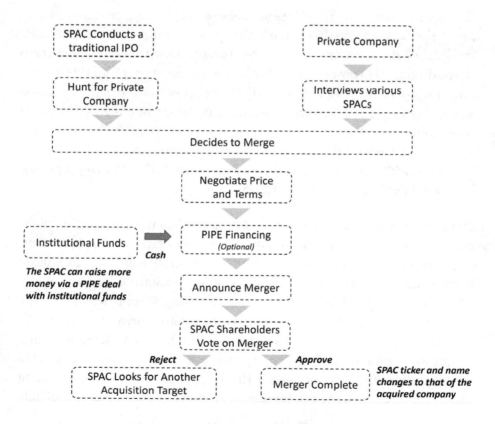

This all sounds great for the buyers of shares, warrants, or both via units, but what's in it for the founders of the SPAC? Founders do not earn a salary, fees, commissions, or anything until the acquisition is completed. Founders use their time and reputation to secure a great company for the SPAC to acquire in hopes that investors will accept the merger. If a merger is successful, the founders of the SPAC get awarded "founder shares" which entitle them to between 1% - 20% of the common shares in the new company. This is also referred to as the "promote". This means their interests are aligned with SPAC holders in terms of looking for a great company to invest in, as they will be owning potentially up to 20% of that company for virtually free. In practice, it is rare to see SPAC founders get 20% of the company; they usually get a smaller percentage anywhere from 1-10%. There is also a lock-up period of 1 year where they cannot sell the stock. It is worthwhile to mention one criticism of this scheme is management's desire to find any acquisition, be it a good company or a terrible one because they want to ultimately get paid. A SPAC has a two year window to find an acquisition, so as that expiration date comes up, they might be incentivized to acquire any company for the sake of completing a deal instead of thoroughly vesting and performing proper due diligence.

SPACs are an alternative to the traditional IPO because it gives a wider set of investors a chance to get on the ground floor of a new stock (they just don't know what company it is yet, but they have an idea of what industry is targeted), with daily liquidity and a guaranteed redemption value. Said another way, if you change your mind at any point, you can sell the stock for $10 before an announcement and if the announced company isn't something you are interested in, you can redeem your shares for that $10. You don't risk losing your initial investment.

From the perspective of the private company: Merging with a SPAC saves time and money. It's a much simpler process because they just need to find one potential investor, the SPAC sponsor, instead of marketing and meeting with multiple institutional investors (hedge funds, pension funds, mutual funds, etc.) to explain their business, talk projections, shake hands, and do a marketing roadshow and Q&A across several cities. The company will raise a fixed amount of money, what's in the SPAC trust, instead of depending on investment banks to tell them how much demand is out there at what price. It takes less time, energy, and money to go public through this route. The SPAC process is much faster than the traditional IPO process, making it easy for a company to go public and to seize a moment when the public is interested in their industry, sector, or product/services offered, thus allowing them to sell shares publicly at the optimal moment and get the optimal (highest!) price.

Private Investment in Public Equity (PIPE)

When the SPAC needs more money than what was raised in the IPO to buy a private company, they find that additional capital in a "Private Investment in Public Equity", or PIPE. In a PIPE transaction, the SPAC identifies an investor or group of investors to provide additional capital to the SPAC in exchange for a private placement of the SPAC's public securities at a price typically equal to the IPO price. This need for additional capital can be the result of two things: 1) the negotiation over valuation of the company the SPAC targeted lead to both parties agreeing to a higher price, and thus the SPAC needs more capital to merge with it, or 2) the company found a larger target than anticipated, and needs more capital to purchase it. PIPEs are allocated to a small group of big investors, usually the same ones that have access to regular IPOs including mutual funds, hedge funds, pension funds, and sovereign wealth funds. And on and on, you get it...the big guys. Investors in the PIPE usually receive their securities at a discount, at least to the market price, and sometimes they even get shares below the IPO price. PIPE shares are sold at a 10% discount or more to the IPO price, according to a recent SPAC study titled "A Sober Look at SPACs" by Stanford Law School and New York University School of Law.

Form S-4 and Pro-Forma Ownership

SPACs need to file an S-4 form with the SEC, which is a required regulatory filing anytime a company announces a merger or acquisition. The S-4 will have a pro-forma, or projected, ownership table listing ownership of all parties involved in the merger. Typically, the SPAC shareholders, the private company shareholders, the PIPE, and the SPAC founders (aka the "promote") are all listed along with their total shares and percentage ownership of the newly combined company. In addition to the S-4, the SPAC will provide an abbreviated version of the S-4 on its website as an "investor presentation". We'll do a deep dive into the pro-forma ownership table in Chapter 21 using the example of Churchill Capital Corp. IV (Ticker: CCIV), which merged with Lucid Motors.

Investment Banking Fees

While the investment banking fees will differ based on the overall size of the deal, the traditional IPO has higher fees than the SPAC route. According to Reuters, investment banks are paid up to 7% of the total offering value on a traditional IPO while larger deals are around 5.5%. In the SPAC route, the investment bank is paid a 2% underwriting fee at the time of the SPAC IPO, and 3.5% when the SPAC finalizes its merger with the private company--effectively bringing that company into the public markets. If there is a PIPE deal to raise additional capital, the bank can earn an additional fee for that work as well. So, is a SPAC really that much cheaper than a traditional IPO? It is hard to say, as every SPAC deal is negotiated at different rates with a multitude of investment banks but on average, the SPAC will cost 5.5% in fees while the traditional IPO will run 7.0%. That 1.5% difference gets slimmer if there is a PIPE deal involved as well. The underwriting fee differential is a reflection of the time spent working on the deals, as traditional IPOs can take years to put together while a SPAC deal takes between 6-8 months. This speedier process to raise capital is another key advantage of the SPAC route.

Let's summarize the pros and cons of a company going public through the SPAC merger route.

Table 3 - Pros vs Cons of a SPAC Merger

Pros	Cons
A private company can negotiate with the SPAC on valuation	Less media coverage
PIPE financing is available for a higher valuation	SPAC founders get free "founder shares" that range from 0% - 20%.
Faster than traditional IPO	PIPE financing sells to institutional investors
Average investment banking fee of 5.5% vs 7% for traditional IPO	Investment Bank cannot pick a group of long-term institutional holders and stabilize price via Greenshoe Option
Broader reach of potential shareholders	No lock-up period for SPAC holders

The SEC Believes SPACs are IPOs

In 2021, the SEC issued a statement equating SPACs to IPOs. While technically different because a SPAC is a merger, the SEC believes the merger between a shell company with a private operating company and is effectively an IPO. But the IPO rules don't apply to SPACs...yet. IPOs are stipulated by the SEC to not provide too rosy or aggressive future forecasts, but SPACs have been doing that to increase investor excitement. According to Bloomberg, the SEC "warned SPACs not to assume they have blanket freedom to publish potentially misleading statements about their future financial performance. He was referring to a legal stipulation that all but prevents companies going public via the traditional IPO route from making similar rosy forecasts. Until now SPACs have interpreted those rules as not applying to them." The SEC believes that If it looks like a ~~duck~~ IPO, swims like a ~~duck~~ IPO, and quacks like a ~~duck~~ IPO, then it probably is a ~~duck~~ IPO.

2020 Resurgence

SPACs became popular in 2020 as a way for companies to go public amidst the coronavirus pandemic mandated shelter-in-place and work-from-home orders that have made traditional IPOs difficult and cumbersome to execute.

As these types of IPOs attract more attention, new SPACs are coming from experienced issuers with name recognition that can attract institutional investors and strong management teams.

Table 4 - SPAC Issuance

Year	Amount Raised ($ in Billions)	Number of IPOS	Average Size ($ in Millions)
2020	41.5	108	385
2019	13.6	59	231
2018	10.8	46	234
2017	10	34	296
2016	3.5	13	269
2015	3.9	20	195
2014	1.8	12	145
2016	1.4	10	145

Source: www.SPACinsider.com

SPACs are more popular than ever. Some of the well-known SPAC mergers include the online betting website DraftKings, space travel company Virgin Galactic, and luxury electric vehicle Lucid Motors.

Table 5 – A Selection of SPAC Deals from 2020-2021

SPAC (Ticker)	Pre Merger Ticker	Merged Company	Business	Post-Merger Ticker
Social Capital Hedosophia Holdings Corp. I	IPOA	Virgin Galactic	Hypersonic and Space Tourism	SPCE
Diamond Eagle Acquisition Corp.	DEAC	DraftKings	Online Gambling	DKNG
Churchill Capital IV	CCIV	Lucid Motors	Electric Vehicle	LCID
Kensington Acquisition Corp	KCAC	QuantumScape	Electric Battery	QS
Altimeter Growth Corp	AGC	Grab	Ridesharing	GRAB

CHAPTER 4

Direct Listing

What is a Direct Listing?

Another alternative to the traditional IPO is the direct listing, also referred to as a direct public offering (DPO) or direct placement. The direct listing path was used by Spotify on April 3, 2018 to go public. Other notable companies choosing this alternative path include the data analytics firm Palantir, enterprise software firm Slack, video game publishing company Roblox, and the cryptocurrency exchange Coinbase. In a direct listing, no additional company shares are created, and no additional capital is raised. Instead, existing shares are sold directly to investors without having investment bankers create new shares and pick new investors to buy them. Therefore, the company does not raise any new capital. The direct listing route gives employees and early investors an avenue to sell existing shares into the public markets right away as they are not restricted by a lock-up period.

A direct listing is a preferred choice for mature companies who want their shares to trade publicly and avoid the high fees of an investment bank to make that happen. Since they don't need capital, there is no reason to pay an investment bank the 7% underwriting fee for their relationships which comes in handy only when you need more cash on the balance sheet.

The Direct Listing Process

While the company still selects an investment bank to work with as an advisor to file the S-1, the company skips the time-consuming marketing effort of a formal roadshow. Instead, they host an investor day and invite all potential investors from mutual funds to retail investors to attend. The investor day is held online and participants get to hear from management and various executives in the company. It's essentially a condensed one-stop roadshow with more access to management and development teams, a product show case, and is open to the general public.

Without the roadshows of the traditional IPO or the merger complexities of the SPAC, a direct listing is a quick way for the company to list its shares and give investors and employees a chance to sell directly to the public. The disadvantage is the risk involved with the process. Notably, there is no support for share sales, no marketing event, no promotion, and no commitment from large institutional investors that promise to be long term holders like there would've been in the traditional IPO process. Remember, the investment banks allocate shares to large funds that promise to be long term holders of the stock so prices don't drop immediately.

With a direct listing, the IPO day proceeds a little differently. Let's take the example of Roblox, the video game maker, which went public on March 11, 2021 through a direct listing. Without an investment bank to set a price range, the "reference price" is often the share price of the last time the company raised additional funds. For Roblox, the reference price was $45. The company's shares started trading on that day after the reference price was set. At around noon eastern time, the shares started to trade and there was a "pop" for a quick gain of 50% and the shares closed at $69.47, up 53% from that reference price that opened trading. According to the online financial database Pitchbook.com, Roblox was briefly the largest direct listing ever, beating out Spotify's direct listing in 2018. Coinbase conducted its direct listing and overtook Roblox as the largest direct listing ever on April 13, 2021 with a reference price of $250 per share.

Exhibit 6 – The Direct Listing Process

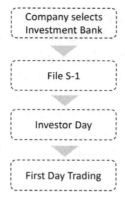

Investment Banking Fees

If you recall, the investment bank usually builds a financial valuation model to determine the price of the stock, calls all of the institutional investors they work with to market the deal, and takes the management team around the world on a roadshow to meet potential investors and tell their story. These are all time-consuming and expensive endeavors, which can be avoided if you don't need to raise new capital. While investment banks charge a 7% underwriting fee for the traditional IPO, the average fee of a direct listing is 2% to reflect the lighter workload. In a direct listing, since no new investors were granted shares, any funds or investors interested in owning the company will have to buy shares on the open market on the first trading day.

Liquidity Event

A direct listing provides a "liquidity event" (fancy word for an opportunity to sell the shares) for employees and early investors. You might ask, if the company is so great why would employees and venture capitalists want to sell shares now? The answer has nothing to do with the sellers thinking the company's best days are behind it but remember these folks have invested and put faith into the company very early on. Employees would like to sell their stocks for several reasons including buying a home, paying for college, buying new cars, and reaping those financial rewards like any investor.

Venture Capitalists have certain time frames to meet and were likely invested in the company very early on. They are obligated to return money to those that invested in their fund by a certain time frame. The liquidity event provides new buyers a chance to invest in the company while allowing early investors an opportunity to convert some of those shares into cash. For every sale, there is a buyer and vice versa, all with their own needs and circumstances so we cannot just assume that employees looking to sell is a negative signal. There are two more notable benefits. A direct listing does not dilute the shareholders by creating more shares and does not have a lock-up period, which requires a minimum holding time for shareholders before they can sell the stock.

The SEC Says "Get That Money!"

However, this all changed on December 22, 2020 as the U.S. Securities and Exchange Commission (SEC) allowed companies to raise capital through direct listings. Previously, companies could only sell shares it already owns to the public. Now, it can create new shares to sell to the public directly to raise money alongside allowing employees and investors to sell their shares. This circumvents the traditional IPO process because companies do not need an investment bank's connections (and high fees) to raise money. The company would be allowed to sell its shares in the opening auction on the first day of trading and raise capital that way. It is believed that a direct listing is better because it allows companies to sell to the highest bidder, whereas the traditional route allows investment banks to allocate (sell shares) to their biggest clients. And if the companies are better at pricing, they will leave less money on the table by setting a price that isn't too overly low.

In summary, here are the pros and cons of the direct listing path to being a public company and how it compares to the traditional IPO.

Table 6 - Pros vs Cons of Direct Listing

Pros	Cons
Market-based pricing of shares determined on the first day instead of Investment Banks picking a price	Can't raise capital (As of December 2020, can choose to raise capital, SEC has relaxed this rule)
Underwriting fees of 2% vs 5.5% for SPAC and 7% for traditional IPO	No Greenshoe Option to protect against a price decline
No shareholder dilution as no new shares are offered	No long roadshow to build interest and market your company
No lock-up period; employees can sell on the first day of trading	
Current shareholders benefit from the IPO "pop" instead of funds that received newly issued shares	

Buying $1,000 of Spotify (SPOT) stock on the day of its direct listing on April 3, 2018, would lead to a cumulative return of 111%, or an annualized return of 31%, turning that initial $1,000 investment into $2,112 as of December 31, 2020.

CHAPTER 5

The Spin-Off

PayPal Spins Off From eBay

Sometimes, a new company is created by leaving its parent's house to make a name for itself. A spin-off is when a company's subsidiary becomes big enough to stand on its own without the financial and reputational help of the larger corporation. A recent example is PayPal, the financial technology company that was spun off from eBay, the e-commerce parent company. PayPal was acquired by eBay on October 3, 2002 for $1.5 billion, in the early days of the internet to help facilitate trustworthy online payments. Since then, it has grown into a peer-to-peer transfer giant, a small business transaction processor, acquired Venmo which provides payment services to apps in addition to being the disruptor to PayPal's peer-to-peer dominance, and recently jumped into cryptocurrency trading and ownership. PayPal has empowered small businesses and freelancers with the tools to get paid for their work. No one wants to be the dinner table accountant when a large bill comes, so Venmo solved that problem. Venmo has made splitting a meal with a large group of friends simple (by requesting payment) and fun (with emojis) by destigmatizing the often awkward "hey…you owe me $24.08 for dinner last week" conversation.

On July 17, 2015, shareholders of eBay received one share of PayPal stock for every share of eBay owned stock in a spin-off dividend payment. The company left on friendly terms, with a cooperative contract in place. But it was clear that PayPal represented the innovative future of financial technology

Can we adapt this for a region like the Temecula wine Region??

(fintech for short) and being under eBay's umbrella hindered its growth. By not exclusively focused on helping the parent company, PayPal was free to grow and work with a variety of businesses that compete with eBay and in industries outside of e-commerce. For innovative companies that are subsidiaries of larger conglomerates, their unique growth and value are hidden by the larger presence of the parent company. Wall street will often talk about "unlocking value", which simply means making people realize the small company held by the larger company is much more valuable separately than it is all lumped together. Said another way, PayPal's value was easier to recognize once it wasn't a part of eBay. Its growth trajectory, business opportunity, and unique profit margin profile afford it a higher valuation. Sure enough, roughly 5 years after being spun off from eBay, PayPal is valued at $274 Billion while eBay is valued at $34 billion, a fraction of its former subsidiary.

Exhibit 7 - eBay Spins off PayPal

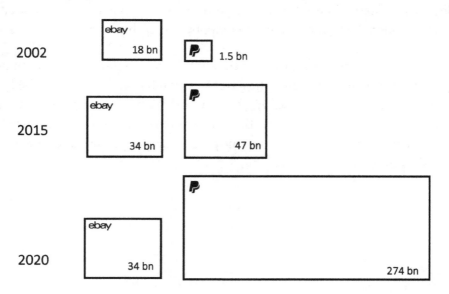

Buying $1,000 of PayPal (PYPL) stock on the day of its separation from eBay via a spin-off, July 17, 2015, would lead to a cumulative return of 538%, or an annualized return of 40%, turning that initial $1,000 investment into $6,380 as of December 31, 2020.

Yum! Brands Goes East

Yum! Brands is the owner of several well-known American fast-food chains such as Kentucky Fried Chicken, Pizza Hut, and Taco Bell. The company is well established in the U.S. but has been growing rapidly in China. In 2016, management decided to separate the China regional segment into its own company, so the company can better focus on winning that market by honing a strategy, adapting menus to changing local tastes, and not being bogged down by a bureaucracy based in the U.S. The China segment had become a bigger and more important factor of growth and deserved its own corporate identity. In 2016 Yum! Brands, with the urging of its investors, issued Yum! China shares to its holders and split the company into two: YUM and YUMC, with 1 share of YUMC given to YUM shareholders in a dividend payout. The China division of YUM had grown up and was ready to chart its own course. YUMC is now headquartered in China and has a large Chinese management team that better understands the regional and local consumers while able to set a course for growth as a separate company, unencumbered by what its parent company might think.

A spin-off is effectively an IPO for the subsidiary, so retail investors can be part of the process by buying the parent stock (eBay and Yum! Brands) before the spin-off is completed. While a spin-off might not receive the fanfare a traditional IPO gets, it is nevertheless an opportunity to invest in a newly public company simply by owning the parent company shares and receiving the subsidiary as a stock dividend.

Exhibit 8 – Yum! Spins off Yum China

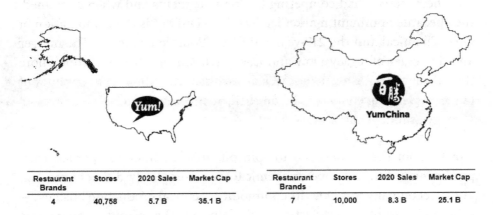

Restaurant Brands	Stores	2020 Sales	Market Cap
4	40,758	5.7 B	35.1 B

Restaurant Brands	Stores	2020 Sales	Market Cap
7	10,000	8.3 B	25.1 B

Buying $1,000 of Yum! China (YUMC) stock on the first day of trading after it spun off from Yum! Brands on October 27, 2016 would lead to a cumulative return of 129%, or an annualized return of 22%, turning that initial $1,000 investment into $2,293 as of December 31, 2020.

1 + 1 = 3

Usually, when you hear about mergers you hear about a large publicly traded company like an Apple, Microsoft, or Amazon buying smaller companies. For example, Facebook acquired Instagram and WhatsApp, two smaller rivals in the budding social media industry. Nike acquired the smaller brand Converse, while Unilever acquired Dollar Shave Club to compete with Proctor and Gamble's Gillette. Coca-Cola acquired Honest Tea to build out a healthier offering outside of sugary sodas.

Let's consider this math equation: 1+1 = 3. Weird right?

Sometimes there is a "merger of equals" where two companies of roughly the same size combine. The combination of Dow and DuPont into DowDuPont created a large conglomerate providing all sorts of chemicals used in farming and industrial production. However, after the merger, the company separated into three unique standalone companies.

Why? Because bigger isn't always better in this case. Dow and DuPont, before their merger, had competing business segments and when combined, they became dominant market leaders. DowDuPont is the combination of Dow Chemical and the 217-year-old EI du Pont de Nemours. The merger and demerger of legacy-Dow and legacy-DuPont has taken a while, more than three years. After that, it was determined that their different lines of business were big enough to be on their own; able to determine their own strategy as independent firms.

DowDuPont then proceeded to spin off three distinct companies, each producing a different type of chemical for a completely different market. The first company was Dow, its commodity chemical production business— think paint additives or plastics made from oil. The second company was DuPont, which will be focused on specialty chemicals—think advanced plastics for electronics and cars. The third company, Corteva, will produce agricultural products like seeds and pesticides.

1+1 = 3.

Dow + DuPont = Dow + DuPont + Corteva

Exhibit 9 - Merger and Spin-Off

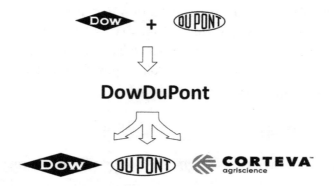

Retail investors would have access to these three new stocks by simply buying Dow or DuPont prior to the merger and subsequent spinoffs. After purchasing the stock, you simply sit back and let the merger and spin-offs proceed.

CHAPTER 6

A Unicorn Goes Public

Image: Designed with resources from Flaticon

Scene:

Three employees of the Unicorn Car Company, a maker of autonomous solar-powered electric cars, meet up at Union Station in Los Angeles near the famous Olvera Street and open the Unicorn app to check in. Spencer "SPAC", David "Direct Listing", and John "Le IPO" (he's French) are waiting for their ride from Union Station to the new manufacturing plant in Las Vegas, a couple of minutes from the famous Vegas Strip. The Unicorn CEO, "Trillion" Tram, arrived at the new Nevada plant earlier to check in on the construction and is eager to hear about the group's ideas for taking the company public.

John: Alright guys, let's get in. Scan your phones and we'll get going.

Spencer and David scan their phones and the Unicorn sedan door swings open; the car's artificial intelligence (AI) powered voice assistant welcomes them. Everyone puts on their seatbelt and the car starts to pull out, passing by the various eateries and shops of nearby Chinatown before entering the freeway onramp.

Spencer: Alright, we're meeting the CEO "Trillion" Tram to discuss the various options we have to take Unicorn public. Tram thinks we're finally at a good spot to do so and I agree. We gotta figure out which option is best.

David: Ok, she tasked us to give her our recommendation and we've been kinda tackling different options. Look, I'm open to different ideas so let's hash it out here and see if we can agree with one recommendation to give her. She's too busy to weigh all of the options and no one likes a two-handed economist. We don't want to come with an option A and say...on the other hand option B is great too.

John: I spoke with the investment banks; it looks like we have a few options. We can do the usual IPO route, we can merge with a SPAC, or we can do a direct listing and start selling shares to the public.

The car senses the hot Southern California sun and dims the unibody glass roof. The shimmer from the solar panels on the roof and trunk disappear as the windows are dimmed. With the windows now almost opaque, you can see a few alerts. The car recommended checking out the highly rated eatery Cielito Lindo nearby. It catches John's attention, so he taps "save" for next time. Air conditioning starts up and the AI assistant asks "Passengers, can I offer you a drink?".

Spencer: But first, coffee. I'll take an iced coffee, please.

John: A lemon sparkling water for me, thanks.

David: Just a Gatorade for me, thanks.

The car dispenses the three bottled drinks from its refrigerator storage unit housed in the front of the car, which sits below the solar panel covered hood of the car. Gasoline powered cars have big engines under the hood, but Unicorn cars have 4 electric engines total, one attached to and powering each tire. A quick glance at the dashboard displaying 90-degree temperature and clear skies along with medium traffic means it's just a typical southern California day.

John: I talked to a few investment banks and I think the traditional IPO route makes sense for us. The largest advantage is a chance to raise some capital for us as we complete the Vegas factory and also think about a factory in Arizona and Texas to build new models, including a truck and maybe an SUV. Beyond our borders, we need to think about having money on hand to build a factory in Europe and Asia so we can sell in those markets. The investment bankers tell me there is massive interest in Unicorn right now; everyone loves the experience of riding with us and the waitlist for our cars stretches years out. They think it'll be a huge hit on Wall Street and can guide us through the whole media circus that comes with it.

Spencer: I'm thinking more clearly with some coffee in my system and that makes sense. I talked to some folks at Lucid Motors and QuantumScape, who I met at CES a while back, and as you know they went the SPAC route. I like the idea of merging with a SPAC because we can raise all the money we need while saving a lot of time. The SPAC has lined up the large funds and rich folks we need to do a PIPE financing if we want a higher valuation. I think the biggest benefit is we don't have to commit the huge resources to make Tram and the management team fly to San Francisco, Boston, NYC, London, and Shanghai on a roadshow to pitch the stock. The traditional process is such a long and involved event that I think it actually distracts us from what we do, which is make cars. We need to focus on getting this Vegas factory up and running ASAP so we can deliver cars on time.

David: Tram is razor-focused on making sure our customers get their cars on time and our AI software packages stay ahead of the competition. Her days are packed with meetings and I believe she should focus on product development like improving food and shopping recommendations, pre-filling the car with drinks that customers love, and keeping the temperature in the car pleasant. I think both the IPO and SPAC processes take up too much time. I propose we go with the direct listing route and get our shares trading publicly as quickly as possible. This frees up time for us to do our jobs without the media circus and regulatory burdens of both. We can talk to the CFO and see if we do need more capital, but the Vegas plant is paid for and isn't done yet. It's a little premature to think about more plants, no?

Spencer: If we pre-fill the car with milkshakes from Chick-fil-A, we'll have 100% market share in no time. I'll keep dreamin' but it's only a crazy idea until it happens.

John: Love their milkshakes. Thanks for sharing your thoughts, these are all valid points. I agree the IPO process will take a lot of time from our executives and Tram won't like it. However, it's a once-in-a-lifetime opportunity, and given how awesome we are, don't we deserve a little attention in the spotlight? She'll get to ring the Nasdaq opening bell and chit-chat with Jim Cramer on CNBC and probably Emily Chang on Bloomberg. We'll have a big party at the office and get no work done that day; it's a win-win. Look, we've all worked hard these past few years to make Unicorn cars the market leader in electric vehicles, over-taking Tesla and the old school U.S., Japanese, and German boomer brands.

David: That does sound fun. The biggest issue I have with the IPO process is how much the investment bankers will take.

John: Yes, it's around 7% of the total capital raised. If we raise $10 billion, they'll take $700 million home in fees. That's steep. Another concern I have is the whole allocation and pricing process, which is in the hands of the bankers. Another drawback we should think about is the pricing. It screams of inefficiency. I did some research and came across Bill Gurley's blog "Above the Crowd". He mentioned that the "pop" will essentially benefit the large funds instead of having that cash go on our balance sheet. The banks aren't going to put a higher, more optimal price out there because they purposely price it for the "pop". The initial IPO range will be determined solely by the banks, without the normal market-based matching of sellers and buyers because we aren't opening it up to everyone who might be interested, including the people that buy our cars. At the end of the day, the shares sold during IPOs will go to the bank's biggest clients. It's a small and elite club of wealthy hedge fund managers. They will get the benefit of the "pop". Look, everything else in the economy has the basic market-based matching of supply and demand. If I want to sell my Air Jordan XI, I'll put it on eBay and let everyone bid for it. If

I want to sell my house, I'll list it and tell my agent I want to see all the offers. I don't let someone else set a price and make it available to a handful of people.

Spencer: SPAC fees are steep too, with the sponsoring SPAC poised to take anywhere between 1% to 20% ownership of the company as part of their "promote" payment. It'll be a long process to interview and figure out which SPAC has the right management team and enough capital to merge with us. SPACs are so new but it seems like all of our electric car peers are doing it. SPACs have gotten a bad rap recently due to aggressive financial projections, large "promote" percentages, and poor market performance after the merger. There has been a lot of shady SPAC deals and headlines calling SPACs the next bubble. The optics aren't great right now. The electric car names have been whacked in 2021. If we decide to go the SPAC route, we'll give the sponsors something like 1%. That's what the largest SPAC deal ever, Indonesia super-app Grab, did with Altimeter Growth Corp. (Ticker: AGC). The good thing is we have room to negotiate and there are so many of these SPACs hungry for a merger, which gives us the advantage when we negotiate the terms. SPAC or traditional IPO--I'm supportive of raising capital because as we ramp up car production, we for sure will need more capacity or simply need to spend more money to pay for things like semiconductor chips, solar panels, and batteries. Never hurts to have more money on the balance sheet, you never know when you'll need it.

David: Fair enough. I will stress again that the direct listing process is just more efficient. We match up directly with any buyers and won't allow the bankers to hand out our shares to their biggest and wealthiest clients. And more importantly, we get the proper valuation, so everyone in this car and our colleagues at the office will get the "pop". We don't have a lock-up period, so we can sell some shares and finally buy the stuff we've been waiting on like a house. I can't argue against wanting to have more cash on hand, but the IPO "pop" is such an inefficient mispricing that benefits only the people we literally gave new shares to that very morning. That's just not fair. We lock out our customers and other investors and hand the shares to a few people who are already pretty wealthy. If we need more cash in the future, I propose we do the direct listing route and then raise that money later, through a secondary offering. It's like a second IPO for public companies where we sell some shares and raise money, but at the current market price in the future.

The car takes exit 246 at Baker, CA and pulls into a preset stop: Alien Fresh Jerky. The team loves the variety of jerky and eclectic alien merchandise. People usually get a few bags, but it goes faster than you think. The team loads up on arguably the world's best jerky and heads towards the car, which senses their approach and starts up by blasting the AC on maximum to deal with the Death Valley sun and 134-degree heat that is prominently displayed on the large thermometer.

Spencer: What flavor did y'all get? I got Roswell Carne Asada Jerky and BBQ on the Moon.

David: Just a few bags of Sweet & Spicy Jerky for me. Still number two behind Buc-ee's, the best jerky in Texas.

John: That's just Texan bias. I love the Extreme Hot Beef Jerky. I literally tear up eating it because it's so hot. How's the car's battery lookin'?

David: Fully charged! The solar panels on the hood and trunk charge our baby as we drive and park. Guys—every time I walk through a parking lot, I love seeing what people are driving. I always see some really sick old school rides on a Vegas trip. It made me realize that in the last 100 years, the only American auto companies to not go bankrupt are Ford and Tesla. We're building cars in America, using the most expensive cost of labor and for the world's most demanding market, so any buffer of cash for unforeseen challenges is just plain smart.

John: The capital we raise can be used for anything really, it doesn't have to be for future factories. We can use it for the development of AI, new software updates to improve self-driving, better algorithms to reduce battery usage, or just plain old school marketing. A lot of people still drive gas powered cars, so we'll have to get ads in front of them and build more showrooms to start building awareness.

Spencer: Hey, I've got an idea. Why don't we put our logo on the Las Vegas Raiders jersey? It's a great way to build awareness for the fact that we're creating American jobs and our cars are built in the good ole U.S. of A.

John: They'll always be the Los Angeles Raiders to me...

David: Their best years were in Oakland...

Spencer: I'll let y'all settle the best Raiders era debate, but I think we can all agree that having the capital raise is prudent business planning. It takes lots of money to build a car; both the hardware and the software. We need all the dollars we can get. Let's center the debate on what is the best option for the company's needs.

David: Okay. We currently have the best AI enabled self-driving, solar powered, electric vehicle. Our competitors are Tesla, Lucid Motors, Fisker, Lordstown, and Workhorse not to mention Ford, BMW, Honda, Mercedes.

John: Don't forget the iCar from Apple and Google's Waymo. Oh oh...and Amazon's Zoox. A lot of very powerful competitors are knocking on the door. Any shortcomings and you know Elon Musk will kill us with a tweet.

Spencer: The hardware is a design and supply chain problem that becomes an assembly problem. We'll need lots of capital to hire the best engineers from around the world and to build future factories for our other form factors like trucks and SUVs. The software for self-driving works well in warm weather climates on the west coast, free from snow and rainy conditions but it underperforms in the wintery conditions of the Midwest and Northeast. We'll need additional investments there to be a viable competitor. Based on my quick back of the envelope calculations, I think if we can get $10–20 billion raised...we could be in a good place.

David: Are there any SPACs out there that can help us raise that amount?

Spencer: That's a big number, even with the additional PIPE financing, most SPACs won't be able to bring in that much money. If that is the capital we're hoping to raise, my vote is for the traditional IPO route. We'll have to spend more time and energy on the regulatory and marketing side with an S-1 filing and roadshow, but we do it just once and maximize the attention on us to raise all the money we need.

John: It just dawned on me. Cash is just like Alien Fresh Jerky, the more you have the better. It's never enough, when you start using it you use it fast, and when it's all gone, you wish you had more. That's how I think about money. And we need all the money we can get if we want to do all the things we want to do well.

Spencer: I agree. Look, the bankers are going to get paid. But they provide a legit service—they are going to help us find all the potential investors around the world who want to invest with us. Usually, these are long-term investors too, right?

David: Right, there is a lock-up period so insiders and employees will be required to hold the stock for 6 months before selling it. It's not ideal for our employees, who have lots of stocks that they want to sell to buy new cars, homes, or whatever. But what's another 6 months? I think they'll be well re-warded for their dedication and hard work when they can sell down the line.

John: So, looks like we have a consensus? We want to go with the traditional IPO route because, despite the regulatory and marketing burden, we're able to raise lots of money with the largest funds in the world. And we need all of that capital because we want to build awesome hardware and software for our cars?

Spencer/David: Agreed.

The car's AI alerts us "We are approaching Zzyzx. This is your reminder to talk about potential ticker ideas".

John: Awesome! I love this geographic reminder function. Zzyzx...as a kid I always thought this was a spelling error and never could pronounce it.

Spencer: It's simply "Zzyzx". Duh.

David: Oh, so that's how you pronounce it?

John: What should our ticker be? Should we go old school and truncate our name like Apple's AAPL and Google's GOOG or do something like Southwest Airlines' LUV ticker? I like LUV; it has more heart and soul. What's our heart and soul?

46

David: We're true to our mission of sustainability, building every component of every car in the most environmentally friendly way possible. We have solar powered panels on the car, we use recycled materials when possible, we create jobs in America, and are reducing pollution with every mile driven in our cars. That right there is our heart and soul.

Spencer: We're honest and real with our customers, employees, and stakeholders. We share product wins and delays. Our CEO Tram tweets back to customers. Can't get more access and transparency than that.

John: Guys, it just hit me. My kids always tag me with the hashtag #TRILL on Instagram every time I buy them pizza or new Yeezys or a PlayStation game. I looked it up on urbandictionary.com once...TRILL is a combo of the words True and Real.

Spencer: I love it. That speaks to our company's heart and soul. Boomers will scratch their heads though.

David: It's fresh and iconic. We're a fresh and iconic company. Let's do it.

John: Tram always wanted the company to have a TRILLion-dollar valuation. She's the trillest person I've ever met. It's all coming together. My vote is for TRILL as our ticker!

The car pulls past the lights and crowds of the Vegas Strip. The targeted ads pop up on the dashboard window...a new steakhouse recommendation for John, prices for a table at the Calvin Harris show tonight for Spencer, and a high roller poker tournament invitation for David. A couple more minutes and they can see the I-beams that form the skeleton of the factory slowly come into view. They are pulling into the entrance of the Unicorn Car Company's Nevada factory and the CEO Tram, in a hardhat, can be seen standing by the designated stop area ready to welcome them.

PART 2

EVALUATING IPO OPPORTUNITIES

CHAPTER 7

My Background & Experience

My Background

Who am I and why should you care what is in my IPO Tool Kit? After all, everyone has a "hot stock tip" these days. Why should you listen to me? Let me tell you my story.

After graduating from UC Berkeley, I worked some odd jobs in San Francisco and Washington, DC but my passion remained in investing. I knew it was what I wanted to do because I daydreamed about it at work. I decided I had to make it happen, so my next step was to pursue an MBA at George Washington University (GW) with a focus on Finance and Investments. The most consequential class at GW, managing a portfolio for the student-run Ramsey Student Investment Fund (RSIF), taught me how to pitch a stock. Our goal was to replace a current stock with a superior one, so I pitched a recommendation to buy Google and sell Intuit. It forced me to debate between two good companies and lay out my reasoning and analysis. We were taught to focus on four areas of analysis: Business, Management, Balance Sheet, and Price. This was known as the BMBP framework. This was the first time I used a structured framework to analyze a stock and my IPO Tool Kit is an evolution of this framework, with my work experience researching stocks and analyzing portfolios contributing to that evolution.

After my MBA summer internship with Calvert Investments, where I interned as an equity research analyst, I knew that I was finally in the right industry. I woke up excited to go to work, always checking the markets for important news. Calvert shaped my understanding of what goes into a portfolio, how to decide what sectors to invest in and, from there, how to conduct research to find the best companies in that sector. This is known as "top-down" research. Let's say you believe the housing sector will do well, because mortgage rates are low, and the energy sector will do poorly because oil prices are low. These are top-down ideas, and research analysts take it from there, researching the best stocks to buy related to housing—home-builders, mortgage lenders, and/or residential REITs. Likewise, analysts would review the energy holdings in the portfolio for anything that is very challenged by low crude oil prices, which drive revenues for the energy companies, for a potential reduction.

At Calvert, I was a generalist who got exposure to every industry. I gravitated towards technology, consumer discretionary, telecommunications, and in particular, loved learning about internet businesses and the rising internet giants in America, China, and India. I was part of the launch of the Calvert Emerging Markets Fund and provided critical information to the portfolio managers, a highlight of my time at Calvert.

As my MBA wrapped up, I flew to Westport, CT to interview with the hedge fund Empire Capital Management. This involved pitching Google, my favorite stock at the time, to their portfolio manager. I didn't own any then, but from the first time I heard about its IPO to my final days of business school, I don't think I went a single day without using a Google service. It was the name I wanted to pitch and the deck was ready to go thanks to my work in RSIF. It landed me the job at the hedge fund.

After graduation from business school, I joined Empire in its new Los Angeles office and was one of five research analysts who reported to a director of research and two portfolio managers. I started as a generalist and, over time, I was assigned to cover the internet, China, and the video gaming industry as these areas represented a combination of my passion and expertise. In 2013, these internet companies were fresh, risky, and had not grown to become the well-known internet giants we know today as the FANG, which is an acronym for Facebook, Amazon, Netflix, and Google (renamed Alphabet). I also covered the BATs, encompassing Baidu, Alibaba, and Tencent which represented the "Big 3" internet giants of China.

Across gaming, I covered Activision, Electronic Arts, Take-Two Interactive, Glu Mobile, and King.com. Some of the smaller companies we analyzed include Twitter, The Lending Club, and RetailMeNot. The hedge fund experience was a true education in using fundamental analysis and trying to marry it with technical analysis. I had to know why the company was investable (fundamentals) and to be able to find the right time to buy and sell (technical) to maximize gains for investors.

The IPO Guy

At Empire, I got to do something I've always wanted to do: research IPOs. As a hedge fund, our allocations were typically lower than those of mutual funds, pension funds, and other larger institutional investors because when an investment bank takes a company public, they want shares to be in the hands of long-only (funds that do not bet against a company) and long-term focused investors. Hedge funds usually get a smaller allocation. After spending some time studying our portfolio, our thematic focus, and what each analyst liked, I got to review my first IPO. I did my best to read the important parts of the S-1, understand the business and its drivers of profit and revenue growth, build a financial model, and prepare to talk to management teams on the roadshows.

I began to deeply study IPOs. Which investment banks were involved in the most IPO deals? How are tech IPOs different from healthcare and other IPOs? Which ones were the biggest? Why do some IPOs flop? Most importantly, which ones were the most successful and how do I identify those? Due to the sheer volume of IPOs, I had to come up with a system to determine which IPOs merited our time and attention.

As I got more involved with the IPO process at the hedge fund, I became more confident and decisive with my analysis. I could arrive at the conclusion of ultimately participating in the IPO or not more consistently after I gave myself a structured due diligence process to repeat. Due to our size and smaller allocation, it was rare for us to hold onto a new issue for long. Another factor was the initial volatility around trading the first few weeks, as the latest IPO was the newest and shiniest toy in the market which got a lot of attention, meaning higher trading volume and price volatility. There were a few IPOs where I made a case to hold the stock for over a year.

I started to think more and more about which IPOs, if held over long periods, delivered the best results. I wanted to use these IPOs as an example and reference point to fortify my case for any future stocks I thought we should keep. As my research progressed, I got to learn about different industries and how the best IPOs told stories of rising trends and globally dominant brands, including McDonald's, Coca-Cola, Nike, and Amazon. In my analysis, I loved to keep it simple and was inspired by the question of "How much would you have now if you invested $1,000 at the IPO?". This was simple because it took day trading and market timing out of the question while allowing me to analyze the company across numerous business cycles. My research allowed me to learn about a company in almost every sector and learn more about the thirteen attributes of a successful long-term IPO buy and hold.

This isn't an exploration of how to best trade and time an IPO, but about which attributes and traits define a great company that you can hold for a long time. It's an active approach to a passive investment because after the initial research, history dictates you leave it alone and let the power of growth and compounding do all the hard work. In a sense, the process of successful investing is as much about knowing history as it is about understanding finance. When you look back you discover trends that can be identified. As Mark Twain said, history doesn't repeat itself, but it often rhymes.

Those rhymes make the best investments, and I'm the guy who loves finding them! I have made it my professional and my personal passion to study what works, what doesn't, and how to make the best educated guess of investing in a new IPO. I'm the guy who wants to talk about this at holiday parties and reads about this for fun. And, I'm the guy who can give you the best tools for your own investing tool kit.

CHAPTER 8

Navigating the S-1 Prospectus

Now that we know about the different paths a company can take to become a public company, you may be itching to get started analyzing the latest IPO candidate. But before you make an investment, we first have to do our research. Where do you even begin? Let's start by going over what is contained in the lengthy S-1 filing document.

www.RetailRoadShow.com

As a retail investor, you will not have access to management teams for a face-to-face meeting during the roadshow. The next best thing, and perhaps a nod to the future, is www.RetailRoadShow.com. This website will provide a list of current IPOs, their S-1 prospectuses in PDF format, and often will have a recorded video of the management team discussing their company's business and culture—major topics that would be covered in the face-to-face process. Through the prospectus and the video, you can learn a lot about a company. The first step is to watch the video and take notes on anything important that is said and catches your attention. It will allow you to tackle the second step, the mammoth 300+ page prospectus document, more efficiently and allow you to research competitors in the space to get a better understanding of where the company is headed.

One thing I wished I had when I started researching companies was a roadmap or tool kit for navigating the S-1 filing (also referred to as the prospectus). The prospectus can be a is a massive document that covers a lot of relevant information, which is a good thing, but realistically no one can dedicate time to reading around 300 pages of financial and legal language without falling asleep. The road map I envision would highlight the most relevant and important parts of the prospectus, so you can use your time wisely and have an understanding of the company, how it makes money, and what the opportunities for growth include. Leveraging my years of experience, I've put together just such a roadmap to help you navigate the prospectus filing and call it the "IPO Tool Kit".

Finding the S-1 Filing

You can pull the S-1 (prospectus) from two sources:

1. When the IPO is active: www.retailroadshow.com
2. Search for it anytime at the SEC's EDGAR website: https://www.sec.gov/edgar

Let's go over the key components of the S-1, drilling down on what can be found in each section and the key things to look out for. In the Tool Kit chapters after this, I will spell out the attributions of a successful company and where in the S-1 to find the data and information needed to form an opinion. For each of the following sections in the S-1, you can simply hit CTRL+F to search for the sections among the hundreds of pages of financial and legal jargon.

Table of Contents

Here is a look at Airbnb's S-1 table of contents. As you can see, there are over 350 pages in total and a lot of information to digest. We'll need to be smart and efficient with our time so we can track down the important and pertinent information needed to help us answer the question: Should I invest in this company? Focusing in on Airbnb's table of contents, I've highlighted the important sections to focus on.

Exhibit 11 - Table of Contents

Table of Contents

We'll spend the rest of this chapter understanding what is in each section. In the following chapters, I'll introduce you to my IPO Tool Kit that highlights the key characteristics to analyze and where that information can be found in the highlighted section of the S-1.

Cover Page

When you download the S-1 prospectus document from www.retailroadshow. com, the cover page will have total shares offered at the top, share class information, and the names of the investment banks underwriting the deal including the all-important "Lead Left" investment bank.

The banks are listed in sequential order based on the role they play in the deal, from most important to least important starting from left to right. The font size of the banks at the top is larger and bolder—they "bulge" out. The term "bulge bracket" refers to the most important investment banks in the top row. The most important bank will appear on the left most side of the top row, known as the prestigious "Lead Left" bank.

This is the managing bank in charge of the syndicate of banks (syndicate is a fancy word for group) and has the final say as to what goes into the prospectus, which clients to meet in which city, and which institutional funds get how many shares. They are called the bookrunner as they literally "run the books" and know which funds have indicated interest and what the allocation of shares looks like. They put in the most work, know the biggest clients, and will get the largest allocation of the 7% underwriting fee for the IPO. While this doesn't have too much impact on our analysis of the company, we often see the bulge bracket banks Goldman Sachs and Morgan Stanley on the biggest and most anticipated IPOs.

Exhibit 12 - Cover Page

65,800,000 Shares

Albertsons Companies, Inc.

Class A Common Stock

This is an initial public offering of shares of Class A common stock, $0.01 par value ("common stock"), of Albertsons Companies, Inc. The selling stockholders named in this prospectus are selling 65,800,000 shares of our common stock. All of the shares of common stock are being sold by the selling stockholders. We will not receive any of the proceeds from the sale of common stock by the selling stockholders.

Prior to this offering, there has been no public market for the common stock. It is currently estimated that the initial public offering price per share will be between $18.00 and $20.00. We have been approved to list our common stock on the New York Stock Exchange, or NYSE, under the symbol "ACI."

Investing in our common stock involves a high degree of risk. See "Risk Factors" on page 26 to read about factors you should consider before buying shares of the common stock.

Neither the Securities and Exchange Commission nor any other regulatory body has approved or disapproved of these securities or passed upon the accuracy or adequacy of this prospectus. Any representation to the contrary is a criminal offense.

	Per Share	Total
Initial public offering price	$	$
Underwriting discounts and commissions(1)	$	$
Proceeds to selling stockholders(1)	$	$

(1) See "Underwriting" for additional information regarding underwriting compensation.

The underwriters may also purchase up to an additional 9,870,000 shares of common stock from certain of the selling stockholders, at the initial public offering price, less the underwriting discount and commissions, within 30 days from the date of this prospectus. We will not receive any of the proceeds from the sale of common stock by the selling stockholders in this offering, including from any exercise by the underwriters of their option to purchase additional common stock.

The underwriters expect to deliver the shares against payment on or about   , 2020.

BofA Securities	**Goldman Sachs & Co. LLC**	**J.P. Morgan**	**Citigroup**

Credit Suisse Morgan Stanley Wells Fargo Securities Barclays Deutsche Bank Securities

BMO Capital Markets	Evercore ISI	Guggenheim Securities	Oppenheimer & Co.	RBC Capital Markets
Telsey Advisory Group	MUFG	Academy Securities	Blaylock Van, LLC	Drexel Hamilton
Loop Capital Markets	Penserra Securities LLC	Ramirez & Co., Inc.	Stern	Tigress Financial Partners

Letter from the CEO/Founder

Let's move on to the more important sections of the S-1 that will give us insights into the quality of the company. The first stop is the Business section of the S-1, which contains a letter from the CEO or founder. The letter from the founder or CEO (sometimes the same person) is definitely worth a full read-through. It is usually less than two pages long, so it is a quick read. Here, he or she maps out their vision and lays bare the philosophy, dreams, and ambitions of the company. You often walk away feeling inspired by their letter. They talk about the company's mission, not just in business, but the company's role in society. There are plenty of cliché statements about all of the above, but notable examples of grandeur promises have come from the likes of Steve Jobs of Apple, Elon Musk of Tesla, and Jeff Bezos of Amazon. These words, while broad in scope, can help you think about whether their investments now and in the future are in tune with the mission they spelled out. In 2012, Facebook went public and here is a snippet of the founder's letter to prospective shareholders.

Exhibit 13 - CEO/Founder's Letter

LETTER FROM MARK ZUCKERBERG

Facebook was not originally created to be a company. It was built to accomplish a social mission — to make the world more open and connected.

We think it's important that everyone who invests in Facebook understands what this mission means to us, how we make decisions and why we do the things we do. I will try to outline our approach in this letter.

At Facebook, we're inspired by technologies that have revolutionized how people spread and consume information. We often talk about inventions like the printing press and the television — by simply making communication more efficient, they led to a complete transformation of many important parts of society. They gave more people a voice. They encouraged progress. They changed the way society was organized. They brought us closer together.

Today, our society has reached another tipping point. We live at a moment when the majority of people in the world have access to the internet or mobile phones — the raw tools necessary to start sharing what they're thinking, feeling and doing with whomever they want. Facebook aspires to build the services that give people the power to share and help them once again transform many of our core institutions and industries.

There is a huge need and a huge opportunity to get everyone in the world connected, to give everyone a voice and to help transform society for the future. The scale of the technology and infrastructure that must be built is unprecedented, and we believe this is the most important problem we can focus on.

We hope to strengthen how people relate to each other.

Even if our mission sounds big, it starts small — with the relationship between two people.

Personal relationships are the fundamental unit of our society. Relationships are how we discover new ideas, understand our world and ultimately derive long-term happiness.

At Facebook, we build tools to help people connect with the people they want and share what they want, and by doing this we are extending people's capacity to build and maintain relationships.

People sharing more — even if just with their close friends or families — creates a more open culture and leads to a better understanding of the lives and perspectives of others. We believe that this creates a greater number of stronger relationships between people, and that it helps people get exposed to a greater number of diverse perspectives.

By helping people form these connections, we hope to rewire the way people spread and consume information. We think the world's information infrastructure should resemble the social graph — a network built from the bottom up or peer-to-peer, rather than the monolithic, top-down structure that has existed to date. We also believe that giving people control over what they share is a fundamental principle of this rewiring.

We have already helped more than 800 million people map out more than 100 billion connections so far, and our goal is to help this rewiring accelerate.

We hope to improve how people connect to businesses and the economy.

We think a more open and connected world will help create a stronger economy with more authentic businesses that build better products and services.

As people share more, they have access to more opinions from the people they trust about the products and services they use. This makes it easier to discover the best products and improve the quality and efficiency of their lives.

Prospectus Summary

We're getting to the meat of the document with the Prospectus Summary, which will give you a quick run-down of the company's revenue sources and competitive strengths and highlight important items including selective financial statistics. "The Offering" section will summarize the use of the proceeds—what the company plans to do with the additional cash raised during the IPO, along with total shares out, trading symbol (Ticker), and when the lock-up expires. The biggest takeaway is what the company plans on doing with the cash raised in the IPO. Prudent things include investing in additional capacity, research and development, building manufacturing or fulfillment facilities for additional growth, or hiring more people to meet growing demand. In Unity Software's prospectus summary, the company gives a concise overview of its complex software business and potential opportunities for growth beyond the core video gaming market it currently serves.

Exhibit 14 - Prospectus Summary

PROSPECTUS SUMMARY

This summary highlights selected information contained elsewhere in this prospectus. This summary does not contain all of the information you should consider before investing in our common stock. You should read this entire prospectus carefully, including the sections titled "Risk Factors," "Special Note Regarding Forward-Looking Statements," and "Management's Discussion and Analysis of Financial Condition and Results of Operations," and our consolidated financial statements and the related notes included elsewhere in this prospectus, before making an investment decision. Unless the context otherwise requires, all references in this prospectus to "we," "us," "our," "our company," "Unity," and "Unity Technologies" refer to Unity Software Inc. and its consolidated subsidiaries.

UNITY SOFTWARE INC.

Overview

Unity is the world's leading platform for creating and operating interactive, real-time 3D content.

We believe the world is a better place with more creators in it. Creators, ranging from game developers to artists, architects, automotive designers, filmmakers and others, use Unity to make their imaginations come to life.

Our platform provides a comprehensive set of software solutions to create, run and monetize interactive, real-time 2D and 3D content for mobile phones, tablets, PCs, consoles, and augmented and virtual reality devices. As of June 30, 2020, we had approximately 1.5 million monthly active creators in over 190 countries and territories worldwide. The applications developed by these creators were downloaded over three billion times per month in 2019 on over 1.5 billion unique devices.

Content built on the Unity platform offers end-users a fundamentally more engaging and immersive experience than traditional static content. Content made with Unity is interactive, allowing end-users to connect with the content and with one another. Content made with Unity is real-time, allowing it to instantly adapt to end-user behavior and feedback. Content made with Unity allows graphics to be expressed with 3D shape and depth, permitting multiple viewing angles, and enabling augmented and virtual reality.

Real-time is not just a part of the end-user experience. Building content on Unity offers creators significant advantages in development compared to traditional content creation tools. Creators can visualize and iterate on their 2D and 3D creations in real-time and collaborate with each other to edit content simultaneously. This can lead to significant reductions in design and development cycle times.

Improvements in computational power, greater connectivity and the proliferation of devices like smartphones, PCs and consoles have enabled an explosion of immersive and interactive content. The gaming industry has benefited enormously from these factors, with over 2.5 billion gamers driving the fastest growing sector in media today.

Unity has built its reputation in gaming, and our scale and reach in this industry are significant. We estimate that in 2019, on a global basis, 53% of the top 1,000 mobile games on the Apple App Store and Google Play and over 50% of such mobile games, PC games and console games combined were made with Unity. Unity's platform helps game developers—from the largest publishers in the world with teams of hundreds, to mid-sized, small and independent publishers, to individual creators—build and operate high quality games, rapidly and efficiently. Unity games can be built once and deployed and operated across more than 20 platforms, including Windows, Mac, iOS, Android, PlayStation, Xbox, Nintendo Switch, and the leading augmented and virtual reality platforms, among

---

Risk Factors

Readers beware, this section is not meant to scare you, but it is very comprehensive for a reason. The section lays out in full detail all possible risks to the company and its future success. This section covers the liability of the investment banks and the company itself should the stock perform poorly. It's a legal hedge on all the grandiose claims made in other sections of the prospectus but presents an honest assessment of the threats faced by the company. No company is bulletproof and without weaknesses, otherwise investing in it would be a no-brainer and require no work. Here is a snippet from Airbnb's Risk Factors section, which highlights the very company-specific Covid-19 impact on the travel and hospitality industry.

Exhibit 15 - Risk Factors

Risk Factors

Investing in our Class A common stock involves a high degree of risk. You should carefully consider the risks and uncertainties described below, together with all of the other information in this prospectus, before making a decision to invest in our Class A common stock. If any of the risks actually occur, our business, results of operations, financial condition, and prospects could be harmed. In that event, the trading price of our Class A common stock could decline, and you could lose part or all of your investment. Additional risks and uncertainties not presently known to us or that we currently deem immaterial also may impair our business operations.

Risks Related to Our Business

The COVID-19 pandemic and the impact of actions to mitigate the COVID-19 pandemic have materially adversely impacted and will continue to materially adversely impact our business, results of operations, and financial condition.

In March 2020, the World Health Organization declared the outbreak of COVID-19 a pandemic. In an attempt to limit the spread of the virus, governments have imposed various restrictions, including emergency declarations at the federal, state, and local levels, school and business closings, quarantines, "shelter at home" orders, restrictions on travel, limitations on social or public gatherings, and other social distancing measures, which have had and may continue to have a material adverse impact on our business and operations and on travel behavior and demand.

The COVID-19 pandemic, which has required and may continue to require cost reduction measures, has materially adversely affected our near-term operating and financial results and will continue to materially adversely impact our long-term operating and financial results. During the fourth quarter of 2020, another wave of COVID-19 infections emerged. As a result, countries imposed strict lockdowns, in particular in Europe. Similar to the impact of the initial COVID-19 wave in March 2020, we are seeing a decrease in bookings in the most affected regions. As a result, we expect greater year-over-year decline in Nights and Experiences Booked and GBV in the fourth quarter of 2020 than in the third quarter of 2020 and greater year-over-year increases in cancellations and alterations in the fourth quarter of 2020 than in the third quarter of 2020. In light of the evolving nature of COVID-19 and the uncertainty it has produced around the world, we do not believe it is possible to predict the COVID-19 pandemic's cumulative and ultimate impact on our future business, results of operations, and financial condition. The extent of the impact of the COVID-19 pandemic on our business and financial results will depend largely on future developments, including the duration and extent of the spread of COVID-19 both globally and within the United States, the prevalence of local, national, and international travel restrictions, significantly reduced flight volume, the impact on capital and financial markets and on the U.S. and global economies, foreign currencies exchange, and governmental or regulatory orders that impact our business, all of which are highly uncertain and cannot be predicted. Moreover, even after shelter-in-place orders and travel advisories are lifted, demand for our offerings, particularly those related to cross-border travel, may remain depressed for a significant length of time, and we cannot predict if and when demand will return to pre-COVID-19 levels. In addition, we cannot predict the impact the COVID-19 pandemic has had and will have on our business partners and third-party vendors and service providers, and we may continue to be materially adversely impacted as a result of the material adverse impact our business partners and third-party vendors suffer now and in the future. To the extent the COVID-19 pandemic continues to materially adversely affect our business, results of operations, and financial condition, it may also have the effect of heightening many of the other risks

Business

This section is a quick overview of the company's business, including customers, suppliers, and sources of revenue. They will also discuss how revenue is recognized and dive into expenses, gross margins, and net margins. Geography is also key; you will get a chance to learn about the customer base and where the product sells in the world. This section is where specific statistics important to the company and industry are shared. For homebuilders, they would share the average selling price of a new home. For digital advertising, they would talk about monthly active users (MAU), and for smartphone makers, they would share how many phones are sold and the average selling price (ASP) of those phones. Every business is unique, and these selective statistics are what management teams internally monitor, so they are shared as a measure of growth and profitability tracking. The most important takeaway is to learn how the business generates revenues. For example, an e-commerce company might charge a transaction fee of 5% of every sale on the platform (a $100 item sold generates $5 in revenue for the company). This shouldn't be confused with Gross Merchandise Value (GMV) which is the total value of products sold, in this case, $100. Revenue is generated in a variety of ways including product sales, service sales, transaction fees, and subscription fees to name a few.

Some business or strategy outlook is usually provided. Often, you'll get a chance to read about management's strategy, adjacent markets to expand into, new geographies around the world, new models of products, estimates of the company's total addressable market ("TAM"), and a discussion about long-term strategy.

This is an important section to read and perhaps reread later to gain a firm understanding of how the company generates its revenue. Even with well-known publicly traded companies, there is a common misunderstanding by the public when it comes to answering the question "what is their business?".

Let's ask ourselves what do we know about two well-known companies: McDonald's (Ticker: MCD) and Hilton Worldwide Holdings (Ticker: HLT).

Let's do a mini thought exercise. Before you continue reading, say aloud or write down what their business is and how revenue is generated.

When I do this exercise with my friends and family, the answers are something like this:

McDonald's: McDonald's is a global fast-food restaurant chain and revenues are generated by selling burgers, fries, and soda.

Hilton: Hilton is a global hotel chain and revenues are generated when people book hotels for vacation and business. They generate revenues from rooms, food, and activities when you stay.

This is a great guess and explains what each individual McDonald's location and Hilton hotel does. But it doesn't accurately explain the business of the publicly traded McDonald's and Hilton Worldwide Holdings. For the public corporations, the answer goes a little something like this:

McDonald's: McDonald's operates a franchise fast-food model, earning a fixed franchise fee and a variable fee that is a percentage (%) of franchisee annual sales. The majority of McDonald's restaurants are owned by franchisees while the corporation owns a small number of locations.

Hilton: Hilton Worldwide operates and manages several brands of hotels, from economy to luxury, for hotel owners. As the operator, Hilton earns a fixed fee and a percentage (%) of hotel revenues generated from the room, room service, and activities. Hilton owns the brand and operates the hotels, but does not own the hotel.

The brands are well known, a result of consistency and excelling at what they do. The two descriptions of the business models are very different. We learned that McDonald's and Hilton actually do not own the restaurants and hotels under their brands, but instead licenses the brand out to franchisees (small business owners). They provide the blueprint to operate the restaurants and hotels and earn a fee each year for that work in addition to a percentage of sales from burgers sold and rooms booked. For McDonald's franchisees, McDonald's runs the advertisements on tv, creates new menu items, designs the tables and chairs, and makes sure the happy meal toys never run out. For Hilton branded hotels, Hilton Worldwide makes sure the bed sheets are luxurious, pillows are fluffy, the room service menu is tasty, and the staff is welcoming. They run the hotel operations for the hotel owner, who pays them a percentage of revenues generated from that hotel.

Management

This is an overview of the team running the company including the CEO, CFO, and various other management positions. The board of directors will be made up of famous names from the industry and outsiders as well. You also want to see longevity from the team as well as experience working for competitors. You can get a sense of the company's ability to promote based on merit when its leaders have committed to long careers at the company. Red flags include family members in positions of power.

Related Party Transactions

We do not want to see significant related party transactions, meaning that the company is doing business with management directly or with its subsidiaries. You want to watch out for companies that conduct business transactions with their employees or have revenues that stem from the subsidiary or parent companies. These could be potential red flags to investigate further. We talk about this in greater detail in the Risks chapter.

Consolidated Financial Statements

The three financial statements—balance sheet, income statement, and statement of cash flow—are found in this section. These statements are assembled by the company and verified and audited by independent auditors to make sure shareholders can trust the numbers. This will give you a peek into the health of the company, how profitable it is, and how much cash is coming in or leaving the company. We'll explore more as we talk about valuation in the tool kit. At a high level, on the balance sheet, we do not want to see too much debt because the company's profits are eaten away by debt expense (interest the company has to pay back for borrowing cash). Debt/Equity and Current Ratios illustrate this. In the income statement, we want to see revenue growth, strong gross and operating margins, and net income growth. With younger companies investing for growth, we might not see positive net income for quarters or even years. With the cash flow statement, we want to see positive cash flow to indicate the company is bringing in cash. However, if the company is growing, we want to see negative cash flow go to investments in research or in physical property to increase manufacturing capabilities.

Glossary of Terms

This section is a miniature dictionary that can help you navigate the language, terms, and metrics that are unique to the company's industry and the company itself. For example, a videogame company such as Unity Software and a cryptocurrency exchange company such as Coinbase will have vastly different terms, metrics, and language. Even for terms they might have in common, they can specify a different meaning or time frame. It's important to note this section and reference it when you don't understand a term in the S-1. Let's look at a sampling of company-specific terminology that you might run across as you analyze prospectuses.

Table 7 – Unique Terminology

Company S-1	Term	Definition
Facebook	MAU	***Monthly Active Users (MAUs).*** We define a monthly active user as a registered Facebook user who logged in and visited Facebook through our website or a mobile device, or took an action to share content or activity with his or her Facebook friends or connections via a third-party website that is integrated with Facebook, in the last 30 days as of the date of measurement. MAUs are a measure of the size of our global active user community, which has grown substantially in the past several years.
Hilton Hotels	RevPAR	***Revenue per Available Room*** represents hotel room revenue divided by room nights available to guests for a given period. References to "RevPAR index" measure a hotel's relative share of its segment's Revenue per Available Room. For example, if a subject hotel's RevPAR is $50 and the RevPAR of its competitive set is $50, the subject hotel would have no RevPAR index premium. If the subject hotel's RevPAR totaled $60, its RevPAR index premium would be 20%, which indicates that the subject hotel has outperformed other hotels in its competitive set.
Coinbase	Blockchain	A cryptographically secure digital ledger that maintains a record of all transactions that occur on the network and follows a consensus protocol for confirming new blocks to be added to the blockchain.

Company S-1	Term	Definition
Roblox	DAU	**Daily Active Users**. We define a DAU as a user who has logged in and visited Roblox through our website or application on a unique registered account on a given calendar day. If a registered, logged in user visits Roblox more than once within a 24-hour period that spans two calendar days, that user is counted as a DAU only for the first calendar day. We believe this method better reflects global engagement on the platform compared to a method based purely on a calendar-day cutoff. DAUs for a specified period is the average of the DAUs for reach day during that period, so 30 days, for example, in the month of September.
Airbnb	GBV	**Gross Booking Value** represents the dollar value of bookings on our platform in a period and is inclusive of host earnings, service fees, cleaning fees, and taxes, net of cancellations and alterations that occurred during that period.
Roku	ARPU	**Average Revenue per User**. We define ARPU as our platform revenue during the preceding four fiscal quarters divided by the average of the number of active accounts at the end of that period and the end of the prior four fiscal quarters. We measure progress in our platform business using ARPU because it helps us understand the rate at which we are monetizing our active account base.

Now that we have the lay of the land and are familiar with the key parts of an S-1 filing, let's be realistic and acknowledge that no one will read every single page in the document. We need to be efficient with our time and look for data that will help us identify potentially great companies to invest in for the long term. Through my years of experience, I've developed a framework that can help me separate the good from the great companies. We'll explore this framework, which I call the IPO Tool it further in the next section.

CHAPTER 9

Research & The IPO Tool Kit

While the S-1 taken as a whole can be overwhelming, knowing where to focus to find the data we need is critical in making the IPO research process efficient. Again, we're not going to be reading the entire S-1 cover to cover. Leveraging the prospectus, my IPO Tool Kit is a checklist of 13 characteristics I use to methodically analyze the IPO and determine whether it's a long-term investment or not. As you conduct research, keep the following list in mind and note where the company is positioned on each one of these 13 characteristics. These are the characteristics that indicate whether a company's stock is poised to see sustained long-term growth and generate strong returns for years.

The IPO Tool Kit is an evolution of the Business, Management, Balance Sheet, Price (BMBP) framework of stock analysis I learned in business school. My work experience, readings, and own investing has informed and helped the framework evolve into the IPO Tool Kit. The analogy I like to use is the Tool Kit is like a complex recipe; think of a Vietnamese pho broth, a rich Indian curry, or a French beef bourguignon that has been passed down from generation to generation and altered and improvised according to the changing tastes and available ingredients of the times. Your interpretation and use of my Tool Kit might be different; you might emphasize certain characteristics over others or ignore a few completely. That is perfectly fine and is expected because I hope you'll mold it into your own unique framework that meets your investment goals.

The 13 Characteristics of the IPO Tool Kit are:

1. Innovative Products
2. Dominant Market Share
3. Win A Category/Solve A Problem
4. Big Profits
5. Total Addressable Market (TAM)
6. Essentials
7. Global Reach
8. Secular Trends
9. Risks
10. Corporate Culture
11. Valuation
12. SPAC Valuation
13. Brand Equity

We'll explore each of these characteristics in the following chapters and I will provide examples of IPOs that met these criteria.

To bring it all together, here is a table that highlights which section of the S-1 might have relevant information on our 13 characteristics.

Exhibit 16 – The S-1 Map

Tool Kit	Chapter	S-1 Prospectus Section
Innovative Products	10	Prospectus Summary Business Use of Proceeds
Dominant Market Share	11	Market and Industry Data External Sources: News, Industry Reports, Business Magazines
Win a New Category/ Solve a Problem	12	Prospectus Summary Business Use of Proceeds
Big Profits	13	Selected Consolidated Financial and Other Data Dividend Policy
Total Addressable Market (TAM)	14	Market and Industry Data
Essentials	15	Business Market and Industry Data
Global Reach	16	Prospectus Summary Business Use of Proceeds
Secular Trends	17	Market and Industry Data External Sources: News, Industry Reports, Business Magazines
Risks	18	Risk Factors Certain Relationships and Related Party Transactions Legal Matters
Corporate Culture	19	Management Prospectus Summary Business Compensation Discussion and Analysis External Sources: Employee review
Valuation	20	Selected Consolidated Financial and Other Data Capitalization
SPAC Valuation	20B	SPAC Merger Investor Presentation
Brand Equity	21	Prospectus Summary Business Selected Consolidated Financial and Other Data Market and Industry Data External Sources: Customer Review, news coverage, magazine articles

On this page, I've provided a blank tool kit checklist. Feel free to photocopy this page each time you tackle an analysis of a new company. Keep old analyses around as they prove insightful over the years, and help you identify where you were correct or wrong. I love crossing things off a to-do list or checking boxes off, it gives me a sense of accomplishment and a sense of permanence. I tack it to my wall to remind me of the progress.

Exhibit 17 - The Tool Kit Checklist

IPO Check List	Analysis
Innovative Products	
Dominant Market Share	
Win a New Category/ Solve a Problem	
Big Profits	
Total Addressable Market (TAM)	
Essentials	
Global Reach	
Secular Trends	
Risks	
Corporate Culture	
Valuation	
SPAC Valuation	
Brand Equity	

Now that we have our tool kit, we can navigate the S-1 with a sense of focus and efficiency. We're not going to be reading every page of the S-1 but instead, target certain sections to glean information on the Tool Kit's 13 characteristics. Let's dive into some IPOs and see which ones pass my rigorous process and meet the characteristics defined in the Tool Kit.

CHAPTER 10

Innovative Products

Three sections that provide detailed information on potentially innovative products include: Prospectus Summary, Business, and Use of Proceeds.

Let's dive right in and use Netflix as an illustrative example.

Is Netflix Innovative?

Netflix started with a mail-order DVD rental service, using an algorithm to recommend content (an early adopter of artificial intelligence technology) and never charging you a late fee. Your queue for the next movie or DVD was saved online. It was novel and innovative and customers loved it. Then in 2007, Netflix debuted the Watch Now feature to allow you to stream the movie instantly. No more mailing DVDs back and forth in the mail. Streaming movies and TV shows free us from the time constraint and burdens of antenna TV. Looking back, it seems so obvious that these ideas would work, but hindsight is 20/20. In retrospect, it is easy to see success, but innovative companies face a lot of doubters and detractors who question their usefulness, viability and need when they're just starting.

Netflix's S-1, filed in 2002, had a paragraph about their digital streaming ambitions. In the Business section, under growth strategy, you'll find the following paragraph on digital delivery:

Exhibit 18 – Netflix's Digital Ambitions

> *Implementing Digital Delivery.* We continuously monitor the development of additional digital distribution technologies. Historically, new technologies, including the VCR and more recently the DVD player, have led to the creation of additional distribution channels for filmed entertainment. We intend to utilize our strong relationships with the studios to obtain rights to acquire and deliver filmed entertainment through emerging digital distribution platforms as they become economically, commercially and technologically viable for those subscribers who prefer digital distribution.

When Netflix was created, they offered something different from the stale movie rental business that required people to drive to pick up a movie, and return it, with penalties if you weren't able to return the VHS (or DVD) on time. There was even a fee if you didn't rewind the movie when you returned it. Netflix started with mail delivery of movies, which was innovative and saved people time from having to drive to Blockbuster. This innovative business model provided tremendous value to customers because it saved them time, headaches with fees, and provided a vast collection of movies.

Netflix's value creation was in reducing the pain points for consumers to enjoy the content. They removed the need to go to a physical location and the pain of late fees, then they removed the wait time and frustration of missing your favorite episode when it aired on TV and made movies instantly appear on the screen. Blockbuster failed to understand this threat and rejected an offer to buy Netflix for $50 million. Netflix continued to add users throughout the years and ate away at Blockbuster's business. The retail movie rental business model required the additional expenses of a physical location and hiring associates to chat about movies, handle cash transactions, and rewind and organize the movies in store.

Disrupting the Disruptor

Netflix disrupted Blockbuster's business model, then proceeded to disrupt its own business model of DVD rentals by mail by developing the Watch Now streaming function. As the name indicates, the future of Netflix was indeed on the "Net" (internet). In 2007, five years after the company went public and ten years after the company was founded, CEO Reed Hastings launched the streaming service and Netflix realized its true potential of delivering movies over the internet. No more waiting for your DVDs to come in the mail and no more dropping them off at the post office or mail-box (like that was hard work). Now you can stream your movie and shows instantaneously, on your computer and other devices, including TV, tablets, and smartphones. The company took advantage of a growing dissatisfaction with cable TV subscription packages that averaged $120 a month for an abundance of channels (200+) and didn't give the customer the ability to control the episode you want to watch or to resume where you left off.

The streaming service launched in 2007, a year in which high-speed Internet penetration also continued to grow. College campuses around the country saw students stream their favorite episodes daily and this continues to ring true as Netflix makes up 15% of all global internet traffic. 2007 saw the launch of another product that would have an outsized impact on Netflix's streaming business—the iPhone from Apple was introduced on June 27. The iPhone and its various iterations afterward essentially put the power of a laptop computer into your pocket and with that came Apps, or programs, that included YouTube and Netflix. This made streaming videos main-stream. No longer constrained to a desktop at home or a bulky laptop, you could now stream anywhere you went. This made Netflix more valuable, as any wait time (at the airport, on your commute, at the DMV, etc.) suddenly became viewing time.

Timing also worked in Netflix's favor as a financial crisis struck the U.S. economy in 2008, with the recession lasting from 2008–2011. The recession caused consumers to be more frugal and look at their credit card bills to try to cut expenses where possible. In addition to cutting back on eating out, expensive car leases, and fancy vacations, the cable bill was cut by prudent customers. Only live sports, including local sports and national sports such as ESPN, made the package a monthly necessity. But with the recession on hand, a $7.99 monthly package was more appealing than a $60 bill from the local cable company. Thus began the phenomenon of cord cutting. In addition to the low cost, the anytime nature of viewing made the product much more in tune with modern life. No longer did a household gather around the TV at the same time around the country to catch a show—it was all about what you wanted to view whenever you wanted to view it.

By now, the company had two innovative products in its short history. The streaming business makes up the majority of its revenue streams as people pay a monthly fee of $8.99 to have access to a variety of shows and movies. The company was first to offer streaming, first to sign up 100 million subscribers, and first to be available in over 100 countries. Netflix has the technology to deliver content and they have a vast library of shows, movies, documentaries, stand-up comedy, cartoons, you name it, that people want to spend hours binge-watching.

Disrupt Again

Netflix disrupted its disruptive mail DVD rental business with streaming. Streaming came with a cost, as Netflix paid the Hollywood studios millions in rights to stream their content. Content is king and Netflix knew that having strong content was important to keep subscribers from quitting their service. Netflix started by licensing shows and movies from Hollywood's major studios but knew that the day would come when the price of that content would skyrocket or worse, become completely unavailable as the studios built their own streaming networks. Netflix began to invest in its own original content, pioneering shows including House of Cards, Orange is the New Black, Stranger Things, and a host of documentaries and comedy specials to span the wide range of interests of its subscriber base. Today, in the U.S. and around the world, movies and shows are streamed and enjoyed by everyone on various devices. Just a few years ago, this would've been foreign and beyond comprehension.

Netflix disrupted its supply chain—the entertainment production studios—by becoming one. Value is also created when you own the rights to the content. The adage "Content is King" in the media industry points to the fact that shows like Friends continue to be very popular in the U.S. and around the world, which means they continue to generate revenue for their creators. Netflix knew where the value was, in the content, because people love captivating shows that they can watch over and over again.

You Missed the IPO, but It's Never Too Late to Invest

At the time of the IPO, it would have been very hard to imagine in your wildest dreams that Netflix would be so successful at the streaming business it would evolve into 5 years later, but it was clear that innovation was in the DNA of the company. Its mission and product focused on removing pain points for the consumer with innovative products that cut costs and fees to make watching videos more convenient and cheaper.

Innovation is hard to predict and hard to see at first. What if you missed Netflix at the IPO but saw that its streaming service would be something that people would love? At this point in time, an investment in Netflix still would have been an excellent long-term investment. Not everyone will invest in an IPO on the first day, because it takes time to build conviction. Put another way, the Netflix at IPO in 2002 and the Netflix that launched streaming in 2007 are two different companies. The former had innovative plans and ambitions, the latter had an innovative product. It's okay to not pull the trigger on an IPO right away and wait until you understand the company better or get more confident about your views as the company executes on its growth strategy.

Exhibit 19 - Netflix Share Price

$1,000 Initial Investment in Netflix (NFLX)

Source: Factset

Buying $1,000 of Netflix (NFLX) stock on the day of its IPO, May 23, 2002, would lead to a cumulative return of 45,095%, or annualized return of 39%, turning that initial $1,000 investment into $451,953 as of December 31, 2020. A $1,000 investment would have given you a total of 66 shares. On Feb. 12, 2004, Netflix issued a two-for-one stock split, so those 66 shares would have doubled to become 132 shares. The company announced another stock split, this time a seven-for-one stock split on July 15, 2015. On July 15, 2015, your 132 shares would have become 924 shares.

CHAPTER 11

Dominant Market Share

Within the S-1, market share data is often provided in the "Market and Industry Data" section. Beyond the S-1, you can do a quick Google search for estimates of the industry's market share and find data from various sources including business magazines, industry newsletters, and analytics firms such as eMarketer.

Dominant Market Share

Most industries have one or two big players with a dominant market share. One of the things I look for in identifying a great company is to see if they are a leader in their respective field, whether that field is streaming music, air conditioning units, athletic shoes, video game consoles, smart phones, online retail, or fast casual restaurants. Dominant market share is a desirable attribute to look for in a company because it means the company can enjoy the majority of profits generated from that industry.

This might be obvious, but let's explore it from the perspective of a firm that doesn't have a dominant market share. That firm is forced to spend more money on research and development, to sell their product at a discount to compete with the dominant market player, and sometimes forced to take the price set by the market leader, instead of setting the price themselves.

Some examples of dominant market share holders include Google and Facebook, the internet giants that dominate the digital advertising industry.

Across search platforms, Google's ads are delivered to you with every query. Across social platforms, Facebook (including Instagram, WhatsApp, and Messenger) has the premier social platforms for you to interact, share, and consume content while delivering targeted advertising. According to eMarketer analysis, Google and Facebook together represent over 50% of the digital advertising market. And yes, they dominate it.

Duopolies

An industry or sector with two dominant players, called a duopoly, is desirable and presents a situation where investing in both the no.1 and no. 2 could prove to be prudent as they reap the majority of the revenues and profits from the sector. Dominant market share is a desirable trait for our IPO investment because implied in that are strategic advantages such as name brand recognition, stickiness to a platform, and safety in familiarity with a certain product or service.

If you can identify the clear leader or have an idea of which of the pair can become the leader, all the better but owning both businesses in a duopoly is also a good strategy. With two dominant players, profits are divided and not pushed to zero by multiple competitors who aggressively compete on price. In a duopoly structure, the technology or brand equity lead is simply too much for new entrants. Duopolies can also see a myriad of different brands that exist under two major holding companies, but don't let that fool you into thinking there is a lot of competition in the market.

A classic example of dominant market share is Coca-Cola and Pepsi, two dominant players in the beverages and soft drinks category. While Shasta provides a lower priced option, and smaller craft soda brands are regionally popular at a premium price point, the majority of soft drinks are sold by these two global giants. They have branched out beyond sugary soda as of late as a healthy and active lifestyle becomes increasingly important to consumers. Both have brands of tea, coffee, juice, and water. Everywhere you travel in the world, you will find a product in their brand portfolio.

Some other examples include:

- Intel vs AMD: Duopoly in the Computer Processing Unit (CPU) industry which provides the processing power to PCs, laptops, and servers that run cloud applications.
- iOS vs Android: Apple and Alphabet have dominated the smartphone operating market with their iOS and Android operating systems, putting earlier pioneers like Palm and Blackberry out of service. They can benefit from the sale of app programs on their App Store/Google Play Store while also selling devices.

Perfect Competition

Sorry for the financial jargon, but this one is worth mentioning. In an environment of perfect competition, every company sells the same thing at the same price. It's difficult to differentiate one company's product from another so they can sell at a premium or establish a brand identity. The gasoline market is a good example of this. Gas is a commodity, derived from crude oil, and sold to the customer at a set price dictated by demand. The oil and gas industry is a global industry that competes to sell its products around the world. Exxon Mobil and Chevron compete with Saudi Arabia's ARAMCO and Russia's Gazprom. Gasoline is viewed as the same product across any brand as it is very difficult for an average driver to notice any material difference. Drivers usually go for the cheapest option or the option closest to them when the gas tank is empty. This market is 'perfectly competitive" and, in some ways, prone to anticompetitive behavior such as the formation of OPEC, which coordinates price fixing by restricting the supply of gas sold around the world. Ultimately, when looking at IPOs or analyzing companies in general, you want to avoid companies in industries like the oil and gas industry because when competition is so fierce that all companies lowering prices to the point of earning zero profits, it leads to weak earnings and weak stock performance.

In the prospectus, three sections including Business, Summary, and Risk factors will have great data points and clues about whether the company is a dominant market share monopoly or duopoly and whether they compete in a very competitive, low-profit industry. These sectors will have a discussion of the company's main business and products and will discuss who they compete against. In risk factors, companies use this section to mention competitors and their products, highlighting how they can lose out to a rival. You'll have to read all three to form an opinion on the company's situation and it is never a clear-cut scenario of whether a company is a market leader or one of many competing firms. In reality, the company is on a spectrum and more likely than not in the middle. We want to identify and invest in one who is a market leader, with near a monopoly market share backed by strong brand equity, global market share, and able to fend off threats from nascent competitors.

Exhibit 20 - Coca-Cola Stock Splits

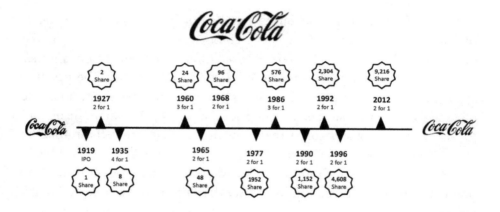

Source: Coca-Cola Investor Relations

Let's revisit our favorite soda. Coca-Cola went public in 1919, so $1,000 back then was a big chunk. Let's keep it simple and assume you only bought 1 share, at $40 per share. Buying 1 share of Coca-Cola stock at $40 per share in 1919 would lead to a fortune worth $19.4 million, assuming all dividends were reinvested into Coca-Cola stock. This represents an annualized return of 14% from 1919 to 2020. What is the cumulative return? Well, it's a staggering 48,500,000%.

Okay wait a minute, most of us weren't born in 1919 and neither were our parents or maybe even grandparents. The internet wasn't invented yet and

I'm not sure if the printing press was either. I know, look—this example is an extreme one to show the power of longevity when holding a stock. Most people think you need 100 or 1,000 shares to benefit from a company's growth, but this example shows that you and your kids, or grandkids, can benefit from just 1 share held for a long time.

CHAPTER 12

Win A New Category/ Solve A Problem

Best Mover Advantage

A company or firm that is first to do something—to offer a new product or service that has not been done before by other firms—is said to have a first mover advantage. They are the first to lay a claim to profits and to establish a relationship with consumers that could be hard for competitors to disrupt. Within the S-1, the Prospectus Summary and Business sections are great places to learn about the company's business and importantly, what problem they are trying to solve. This will help to evaluate whether they have the potential for a first mover advantage.

Some often-cited examples of first mover advantage include Facebook and Alphabet's Google search engine, even though in both of these cases they weren't exactly the *first*. Facebook wasn't the first major social media website—MySpace.com was. Google was not the first search engine, or the second or third. But Facebook and Google offer the best products/services within a new category or industry—in this case, social media and internet search. Being first doesn't guarantee success but being the best relatively early on can help you win the category.

Facebook and Google represent the best versions of social media and internet search because Facebook provided a simple interface to connect to friends, and Google presented a simple results page in response to internet queries. Best, not first, wins categories. Best, not first, solves the problem and creates value.

Intuit CEO Brad Smith wrote in *Harvard Business Review*: "We sometimes joke about how instead of having the first-mover advantage, Intuit had the 47th mover advantage." He was referring to the 46 companies providing finance tracking software when they launched Quicken. Best, not first, wins users and creates customer loyalty.

Electric Cars

Tesla, the electric vehicle maker, was the first new automotive company to form in the last 100 years and was the first to successfully challenge gasoline powered vehicles with its all-electric Model S. Tesla created a new category of electric vehicles (EVs). This new category came as climate change caused by emissions became more important to citizens of the U.S. Gasoline, with its pollutant after effects and dependency on crude oil from the Middle East, made the U.S. vulnerable to governments with policies that do not line up with its interest and values. Tesla's Model S was a car that didn't depend on a single drop of gasoline. A clear break from hybrids before it because you never had to fill up a tank of gas. Tesla's successful launch of the Model S was driven by the company's focus on design, engineering, and marketing. The car had broad appeal as it looked like a combustible engine car but performed well and boasted interior technology that was second to none. Tesla came to dominate the new category of electric vehicles and entrenched itself as the premier leader of the category.

To take a significant lead in this new category and ensure the success of its EVs, Tesla built a network of recharging stations for their car. While gas stations are everywhere, there were no electric charging stations. Tesla cars would need a charge every 300 miles, so without a network of stations, a car owner would be limited in how far they could travel. As the first mover in a new category, its long-term vision and investment in the charging network allowed it to sprint ahead of the competition. This network became a competitive advantage and an economic moat, protecting the company from competitors who do not have similar charging networks. The legacy automakers would look at the cost of building out a charging network as too burdensome and expensive, and would not do it, thus leaving the door open for Tesla to come in and define the new category.

New categories are hard for entrenched companies and it isn't as simple as switching out a v-6 gas powered engine for an electric engine (or 4 because each wheel has its own engine). The new category of EV requires research and development investments in battery, electrical engineering, and a whole new car design that would take time and energy away from the core business of gas-powered car companies. It also required putting in the capital needed to build out the charging network, something that takes a lot of time and resources away from the core business of designing gasoline cars. For all of these reasons, the General Motors, Fords, and Hondas of the world never launched their own EVs. They are legacy vehicle makers that come with liabilities such as pensions for employees that depend on profits that could be eaten away with an investment in EV.

Companies that create and define a new category do not come along very often. They are rare because it is a difficult feat to undertake and there is a low probability of success. When you identify a company that has a compelling product, in a new category, and has a sustainable moat around it, it's definitely a worthwhile investment.

Peter Thiel's *Zero to One* was published in 2014 and greatly inspired me to look for these pioneering and innovative first movers (or best movers) to invest in. The title of his book refers to companies that change their category or industry count from 0 to 1 because they are the very first ones to do it. Copycats and duplicators come later, and then the category goes from 1 to n (many of infinite). One prominent example is PayPal, the first online payment network that powered eBay's payments. They were the very first and created new industries or sub-industries, enjoying the benefits of customer mindshare, brand recognition, innovation advantage, and all the benefits of being a "first mover." You know the story, eBay acquired PayPal and spun it off later as it was clear its destiny was much bigger than being an eBay subsidiary.

Buying $1,000 of Tesla (TSLA) stock on the day of its IPO, June 29, 2010, would lead to a cumulative return of 14,669%, or an annualized return of 61%, turning that initial $1,000 investment into $147,692 as of December 31, 2020.

In summary, let's try to concisely sum up the problems these businesses solve. We can write it into our analysis in the Tool Kit checklist.

Table 8 – What Problem did they solve?

Company	What problem did they solve?
Intuit	Made filing taxes online easy and accessible
Tesla	Solved the problem of mileage range and charging stations for electric cars
PayPal	Solved the problem of payments when buying and selling from strangers online

Thought exercise: Pick three companies that you recently purchased something from and write a single sentence explaining what problem they solve in your life.

CHAPTER 13

Big Profits

A Profitable Business Model

When Facebook went public on May 18, 2012 at $38 per share, it was ridiculed for its massive valuation at around $100 billion. Social media was new to most people in the U.S. and the world. Sure, MySpace.com and other social networks came and went before it, but Facebook was the first to be wildly successful and addictive with over 1 billion users worldwide. First signing up college students, then high school students, and then a generation of parents, aunts, and uncles, friends from elementary school, and ex-boyfriends and girlfriends. A lot of people were skeptical of Facebook's business model of selling advertisements, but it turns out that it is incredibly profitable. First of all, let's try to get a better understanding of social media's business model. In the S-1, the Business section will be the best place to get a breakdown of how the company generates revenues and what its expenses are. The Selected Consolidated Financial and Other Data section will be the place to find quarterly and annual financial data.

Facebook sells advertising that is placed in your newsfeed (they call it native ads) along with advertising on the right-hand side of the homepage. Every time the ad appears on our screen (an impression) or every time you click on an ad (click or conversion), Facebook earns a small fee from the advertiser, such as Coca-Cola, Proctor & Gamble, Nike, or smaller businesses because anyone can advertise on Facebook. We go on Facebook because we want to see what our friends and families are up to, what they eat, where they vacation, what they have purchased, etc. This is the "content" on Facebook and it is provided 100% free by us, the users. Collectively, as billions of users, we consume things that are posted by our friends and Facebook simply places ads between every few posts to keep the ads from being overly annoying. They typically show an ad once every 5 posts, in financial terms this is an ad load of 20%. The cost of goods sold (COGS) for Facebook is a staggeringly low 19%, content is virtually free so the other costs include servers and engineers to deliver all the comments, pictures, links, and videos to the newsfeed. The gross margins (Revenue - COGS) are very high at around 81%, making this an incredibly profitable business. The COGS at digital advertising rival Google is more than double that of Facebook, at $0.47 for every $1 of revenue generated.

Exhibit 21 – Cost of Goods Sold (COGS) at Facebook and Google

$0.47

$0.19

Image: Designed with resources from Flaticon
Source: Alphabet and Facebook 10-K filings.

The more time you spend on Facebook and its family of apps, the more content you consume, the more ads are delivered to you, and the more revenue Facebook can generate. As Facebook became a tool for social connectivity, news consumption, sharing the latest in music and fashion, etc. it became an indispensable part of everyday life.

We often think about Facebook's products as their comments, updates, pictures, and videos but that is wrong. We, the billions of users, are Facebook's product and our *attention* is sold to advertisers who want to sell us products and services. Our profile, what we like and dislike, etc. are sold off to companies who want to advertise to us. Our attention costs advertisers $0.02 per view. Whenever something is a free service, and you ask yourself how do they make money, just know that you are the product.

A business model where content (COGS) is provided for free by users and then consumed by those users is massively profitable. Facebook is simply a middle-man for me to send photos to my family and friends, with an ad inserted in the newsfeed for every fifth status update. This business model makes for a wildly profitable company and a very attractive IPO.

Buying $1,000 of Facebook (FB) stock on the day of its IPO, May 18, 2012, would lead to a cumulative return of 614%, or annualized return of 26%, turning that initial $1,000 investment into $7,145 as of December 31, 2020.

Let's save Google for the next chapter.

CHAPTER 14

Total Addressable Market (TAM)

The Bigger, the Better

A company whose products or services can be used by a large population of consumers or corporate customers is said to have a large Total Addressable Market (TAM) and a major opportunity to grow revenue and profits for long periods of time. TAM is used in finance, and especially in investment banking, to talk about the total opportunity of a company's end market. The figures and statistics you'll need to calculate TAM are often found in the S-1's Market and Industry Data section.

TAM can seem like a complex and deeply scientific number to arrive at, but it's actually really simple and can be done by a quick back-of-the-envelope calculation. TAM is usually quoted as an annual number, as in how much revenue can be generated from serving that particular market within a 12-month period.

Break out the Calculator (Or a Calculator App)

What is the TAM for smartphones?

The U.S. has 300 million people, and roughly every 2 years a new phone is purchased (or 1/2 of the population upgrades their phones each year), and an average phone costs $500. Our simple back-of-the-envelope math looks like this: 300 Million x 1/2 x $500 = $75 billion is the Total Addressable Market (TAM).

What is the TAM for coffee purchased at a cafe?

The U.S. has 300 million people. Let's assume 1 in 10 buys a coffee each day, it can be hot or iced coffee. Let's assume they buy coffee 5 days a week (coffee addicts who can't start the day without it). And let's assume their cup of joe costs $3.00 on average.

300 million x 1/10 buys coffee x 5 cups x 52 weeks x $3 per cup = $23.4 billion TAM for coffee purchased in a cafe.

Industries with large TAMs usually have several successful competitors who provide differentiated products (automobiles) and undifferentiated products (gasoline for those automobiles). Large TAMs can support multiple successful competitors because every person in every corner of the world could be a potential customer (and revenue source), without the brutal dynamics of having a winner-takes-all situation where only the biggest and largest firm reaps the majority of the profits.

Netflix

Remember Netflix, our example from the previous chapter? I think of Netflix's TAM as everyone who has a TV, laptop, iPad, or iPhone because those are all devices on which you can access Netflix via an app. Since you only need one account to log in to any of these devices (and to share with your friends...we all do it), let's keep this TAM example simple. Let's say the TAM is everyone who has an expensive cable subscription with thousands of channels but can never find something they want to watch. Our TAM is a subset of that group that is fed up with paying over $100 a month. There are 150 million U.S. households, but some research leads us to Nielsen data that states 120 million households have televisions. I know you don't need a television to watch Netflix, but let's keep it simple and say if anyone is interested in Netflix, they would at least have a TV in the first place. Okay, so the TAM for Netflix is very simple. It's the $120 million households with TVs. This is conservative because Netflix can reach beyond 120 million through other channels (pun intended) such as PCs, laptops, smartphones, and tablets.

Automobile

The automobile industry is a great example of a large Total Addressable Market with a lot of players providing very differentiated products to a large population of customers. Let's start with car types where we have sedans, trucks, wagons, sport utility vehicles (SUVs), vans, mini-vans, recreational vehicles (RVs), etc. For corporate customers, there are trucks, semi-trucks, tractors, delivery vehicles, coach buses, etc. This is a market where every vehicle type serves a specific need when it comes to transportation based on what you are moving around and how long you need to travel. With a large variety of uses, there are many different companies to meet consumer needs. Honda, Toyota, Ford, General Motors, Ferrari, and BMW are some well-known car makers. Freightliner, Kenworth, Peterbilt, Volvo, Mercedes are some of the well-known brands that make semi-trucks and big vehicles for corporate clients. And of course, we can't leave out our fictional self-driving, milkshake-making Unicorn Car Company from Chapter 6. Overall, the automotive industry has a large TAM because there are a lot of customers and a myriad of different needs, meaning ample opportunity to differentiate from your competitor.

Gasoline

With a large TAM for vehicles comes a large TAM for fuel. For a majority of households, they'll refill their tank about every 2 weeks. They do so without much brand loyalty and will usually buy the same grade of gas but at different stations, based on the location with the lowest price. The gasoline market is a big TAM, but there is largely zero differentiation as gasoline is a commodity without an opportunity to differentiate. Unlike the car itself, with different types, brands, models, and features, gasoline is hard to differentiate beyond pricing. It does remain a large TAM, but the nature of it is different. Cars last 5–10 years, a gallon of gas can last 5–10 days.

Google

When looking at IPOs, identify the TAM and evaluate whether it's a big or small TAM. We prefer big TAMs as there is more opportunity to win a larger pie (total revenue) while leaving room for competitors to come in. A big TAM can be successful for products that are differential or a commodity, but a small TAM means even the best firm with the best product or service might reach its plateau and serve the market quickly. We do not want that, as we want years and decades of growth ahead to meet the needs of a large TAM.

Google, now named Alphabet, went public on August 14, 2004 at $85 per share. The company sells advertising based on internet search queries, which was a growing market at the time but wasn't a big TAM. It had the potential to be a big TAM as internet adoption increased in the U.S. and across the globe. Google was not the first nor was it the only search engine, but it has established a reputation as being the best—able to deliver relevant links and content based on its proprietary algorithm. Google was the best in a crowded field of internet search engines, but TAMs provide an opportunity for the best of breed to capture the majority of the revenues and profits from that industry.

Google's revenue and profits grew as the world went online. The internet became cheaper and more available. It became part of our daily lives as we read emails, check the weather, digest the news, shop online, and search for information. A large TAM is great but a growing TAM is even better. Google was the best search engine for a growing group of internet users. Its business model, to serve advertisements based on every query, meant that every time someone searched on its engine, they could sell advertising space to a marketer trying to get your attention. What's Google's TAM today?

3 billion people online x 5 search queries per day on mobile or PC x $0.02 per query x 365 days per year = $109.5 billion.

With a massive internet advertising TAM of close to $110 billion, a company able to grab a lion's share of the revenues and profits would yield a very successful investment. Google went on to provide services for everything one can do on the internet: search for restaurants and get directions, email, watch videos, and shop. To this day, the majority of its revenues and profits come from internet search, which hasn't reached all of the world's population yet. With the proliferation of PCs, then laptops, then smartphones and tablets, Google has multiple access points to meet your search needs and has become a dominant internet technology company—"to Google" has become a verb in the English language. It all started with providing the best search results for internet queries (best mover), which was and is a big Total Addressable Market.

Alphabet was originally named Google. Buying $1,000 of Alphabet (GOOG) stock on the day of its IPO, August 19, 2004, would lead to a cumulative return of 3,369%, or an annualized return of 24%, turning that initial $1,000 investment into $34,694 as of December 31, 2020.

Just for fun, here are a few more TAM exercises to quickly think through:

1. How many shoes are sold annually in the U.S.?
2. How much is spent on groceries each year?
3. How much is spent on video games in the U.S. annually?
4. How much is spent on food delivery annually?
5. What is the total market for baby care annually?
6. What is the total market for weddings in the U.S.?
7. What is the total value of all homes sold in the U.S. each year?
8. How much does the U.S. spend on new cell phones each year?

CHAPTER 15

Essentials

Burgers, Fries, and a Soda

Essentials are services or products that start out as luxury items (discretionary spending) and over time become a necessity as their usefulness and enjoyment are so great that they become embedded in everyday society.

Another attribute that makes for a great investment, at the IPO stage or at any point in your research of a stock, is if the company sells a product or service that is essential to everyday life. These products or services might be new or have been around for a while, but trends in lifestyle or demographics increase their use as we increasingly value them. Within the S-1, the Business section and Market and Industry Data section will be great starting points. More importantly, external sources such as magazines and newspaper articles can give you great insights into trends and popular products and services.

Let's look at an example. In the years after World War II, known as the post-war era, the advent of fast food epitomized by the rise of McDonald's captured the change in America's eating habits. Women, who filled in for men while they were off in theaters of war in Europe and Asia, stayed in the workforce after the war ended. As American soldiers returned from war and women remained in the workforce, the economy boomed. Women's changing role in society meant a focus on career and less time at home, reducing time spent cooking full meals, which made fast food convenient and time saving. While fast food wasn't invented then, it became essential as both parents worked and couldn't cook dinner every night or lunch for the next day. Burgers, fries, and soda became an all-American tradition and McDonald's helped pave the way for fast food in the U.S. and then across the globe.

Proctor & Gamble

Think of all the items you buy every few weeks to restock your bathroom, pantry, and cabinets. They include everyday essentials like shaving cream, toilet paper, razors, shampoo, conditioner, body soap, and feminine products such as pads. These are items that you need in both good and bad times. They are essentials you refill every time you run out. These items, known as consumer staples, were once a luxury in the U.S., but as American incomes rose, staples became essential to everyday life to maintain a higher standard of hygiene and appearance. Without it, you wouldn't be presentable outside of your own house.

Exhibit 22 - Bathroom Essentials

Image: Designed with resources from Flaticon

America's standard of hygiene started to influence the rest of the world. Now, a rising middle class in Asia, Latin America, and Africa aspire to use these very brands we consider essential. An example of a conglomerate that owns these very well-known brands is Procter & Gamble or simply "P&G". The company is based in Cincinnati, Ohio and has a long history of innovating and acquiring the leading consumer staples brands to build a portfolio of products that we interact with throughout the day. From the moment we rise, brushing our teeth and shaving, to bathing with shampoo and soap, to washing our clothes, or putting on moisturizing cream before bed, we interact with P&G and its brands more than we realize.

P&G stock opened at $100 on Jan 13, 1978. The company is home to well-known global brands including Gillette, Tide, Pampers, Always, and Charmin to name a few. An average American interacts with their brands at least once a day, making it an essential part of life. When a brand is essential, it makes for a compelling investment and Proctor & Gamble has rewarded its shareholders handsomely. The company is known to be a master of marketing.

Here is our definition once again: Essentials are services or products that start out as a luxury (discretionary spending) and over time become essential as their usefulness and enjoyment are so great that they become embedded in everyday society.

Just for fun, can you think of something within your lifetime that was a luxury and evolved into an essential?

Buying $1,000 of McDonald's stock on June 1, 1972 would lead to a total return of 31,293%, or an annualized return of 13%, turning that initial $1,000 investment into $313,926 as of December 31, 2020.

Procter & Gamble went public in 1950, but I couldn't find reliable data going back that far. This was before the data availability we enjoy today, mind you. So, let's look at data when it was available, from 1972 and beyond. Buying $1,000 of Procter and Gamble stock in 1972 would lead to a total return of 11,030%, or an annualized return of 10%, turning that initial $1,000 investment into $111,296 as of December 31, 2020.

CHAPTER 16

Global Reach

Global Consumer Base

As the world has globalized, supply chains and customer bases are now more integrated than ever. Companies with a global customer base are advantaged for several reasons. In the Prospectus Summary and Business sections of the S-1 is where you'll find data on international markets, both current and those planned for future expansion.

With a customer base that spans the whole world, a company's revenue source is diversified and steadied, hedged against any dramatic drop in demand from a specific region. The diversified revenue base will help the company offset weaker sales in any one geographic area and provide a smoother trend line of sales and sales growth. For example, if Europe is in a recession, shoe and apparel maker Nike is not wholly dependent on any one country in Europe nor is it dependent on the entire 27-member European Union. Nike has diversified into other markets including the U.S., China, Japan, Asia, the Middle East, and Africa to continue to reach consumers to buy its shoes, clothes, and accessories.

Often, a global consumer base is complimented by a global supply chain. When a company does not depend on a single country, region, or supplier for key parts or manufacturing, they hedge any risks that might beset those critical suppliers. Supply chain shocks can come in many forms, including weather, political changes, or regulatory changes. Weather or natural disaster shocks, such as hurricanes or storms that shut down factories, can come unpredictably. Western Digital, a maker of hard drives found in computers and laptops, had a majority of its production in Thailand. When regional flooding inundated their plant in 2011, they shut down, causing a global shortage of hard drive parts. Political changes can also affect the terms of trade and make your products harder or more expensive to export. Likewise, regulatory changes can add additional financial burdens to your firm or make securing key materials more difficult.

Nike has a sophisticated supply chain across the U.S. and several Asian countries to meet the brand's massive global demand. Nike's products appeal to the active and healthy lifestyle ambitions of the growing population in the developed world and deploy well-known athletes—including Michael Jordan, Cristiano Ronaldo, Lebron James, Serena Williams, Rafael Nadal, Neymar, Tiger Woods, and many more—to advertise its products.

A globally appealing product is needed to win a diverse audience across different languages, cultures, and income levels. A global customer base forces your development and design team to build a product or service that transcends languages and cultures to appeal to a broad base population. The brand name, the logo (anyone around the world will recognize the famous Nike swoosh), and the product must stand the test of time and be well known to those beyond your country's borders.

Nike went public on December 2, 1980. Buying $1,000 of Nike stock on the first day would lead to a total return of 124,382%, or annual returns of 19%, turning that initial $1,000 investment into $1,244,815 as of December 31, 2020.

Just for fun, what are some brands you can think of that have global reach?

CHAPTER 17

Secular Trends

First and foremost, what does "secular trend" even mean? Let's give it a formal definition and then dissect:

> *"Secular growth occurs when something fundamentally changes within a sector or industry, creating a wave of new demand. Secular growth rates can be materially higher than cyclical growth rates, as secular growth depends on changes in customer behavior rather than changes to GDP."*

Source: James L. Callinan, Osterweis Capital CIO

Given all the successful IPO attributes we've reviewed so far, we know the world is changing and capitalism benefits from a process called "creative destruction," a phrase coined by economist Peter Schumpeter. This is the process of new companies rising to conquer new markets, industries, and revolutionizing the way we consume and live in ways thought unimaginable. In this process they destroy older, slower to adapt companies forcing them into bankruptcy or irrelevancy. It is also known as the theory of "economic innovation and the business cycle". Companies that are on the rise and displacing older ones benefit from a secular trend that plays out over a long period of time.

Let's try to Identify a secular trend that represents a significant change in society. It can be a change in consumer preferences or behavior, or it can be a change in corporate needs and actions that point to a change in the market because businesses ultimately serve a customer. Reading and learning about secular trends give us foundational knowledge. We then try to find companies or IPOs that address that secular trend. Within the S-1, clues to secular trends can be found in the Market and Industry Data section but external sources such as news articles are also great at identifying secular trends.

What are some of these key secular trends to look out for? Next, we'll review several major trends that will impact Americans, citizens of the world, and the earth in the coming years. Companies that solve these problems will be able to get consumer dollars, generate earnings, and be future giants that displace old stubborn rivals that fail to adapt.

E-commerce

One secular trend I would like to focus on is e-commerce. The shift to online purchasing started two decades ago, with eBay and Amazon leading the charge in the U.S. Online purchases still make up less than 20% of retail shopping in the U.S. and even less around the world, where e-commerce is only starting to become more accessible to a rising middle class. Companies that provide a great online shopping experience will save people time and win a large percentage of consumer wallets.

According to data from analytics firm eMarketer, e-commerce is poised to grow rapidly around the world as a growing middle class in developing economies adopt online shopping. Developing markets in Asia, Latin America, the Middle East, and Africa are leapfrogging the retail brick and mortar stores and choosing to shop online instead. In 2020, their adoption was sped up by the Covid-19 pandemic, which forced everyone around the world to depend on e-commerce as shelter-in-place and work/socialize/shop at home mandates made shopping in person less practical.

Exhibit 23 - E-commerce Growth Rate by Region, 2020

Region	Growth Rate
Central & Eastern Europe	21.5%
Middle East & Africa	19.8%
Latin America	19.4%
North America	18.1%
Western Europe	16.9%
Worldwide	16.5%
Asia Pacific	15.5%

Source: www.eMarketer.com

According to Barron's, local e-commerce firms are winning against the American giant Amazon in their home markets. In a recent article, Barron's highlighted two reasons: 1) localized knowledge of customers' needs and 2) better dealing with regional challenges that made these smaller companies the leader in their respective markets.

Table 9 – E-commerce Around the World

Company	Ticker	Region	Secret Sauce
Amazon	AMZN	USA, EU, UK, Canada	Quick delivery, large selection, Prime member benefits
Alibaba	BABA	China	Large selection, low prices
Sea Limited	SE	Southeast Asia	Merchant friendly, monthly sales, low prices
Mercado Libre	MELI	Latin America	Collect Cash upon Delivery
Jumia	JMIA	Africa	Deal with logistic challenges of Africa
Ozon	OZON	Russia	Deliver across a large landmass
Coupang	CPNG	Korea	Same day delivery, reusable containers

Some other major secular trends that are transforming the world are:

1. **Healthier lifestyle** - After decades of consuming sugary soda, fast food, and a lifestyle of sitting the majority of our lives (in traffic, at the office, and finally in front of the TV at home), Americans and other developed nations have a host of health complications with their heart, weight, blood pressure, you name it. Companies that can promote a healthier lifestyle through nutrition, exercise, or a lifestyle change will be important and could be a viable investment if they pass the rigors of the IPO Tool Kit analysis.

2. **Meat alternatives** - As the emerging markets of the world (think China, India, etc.) grow their middle class, there is an increased appetite for meat protein. Beef, chicken, and pork are highly desirable but require a tremendous amount of resources to produce—land, feed, transportation—all contributing to a big carbon footprint. There has been a rise in alternatives to meat that taste, feel, smell, and look like meat but are made from vegetables or other ingredients. These companies will generate revenue and profits by filling the gap in supply as the world's appetite for red meat won't be met by current supply chains.

3. **Streaming television and music** - While it might be more common in the U.S. and the wealthier nations of the world, streaming

television, movies, and music is still in the early stages of taking over the traditional airwave and cable delivery methods of TV and music globally. While the U.S. might be first and ahead in the area, countries around the world are adopting streaming products more slowly. The early winners include Netflix, Spotify, Disney+, YouTube, etc. but this secular trend is still early on in its life and there are many more eyes and ears to serve, meaning the potential revenues and earnings are massive.

4. **Global climate change** - The earth's climate is getting warmer, which has wide-ranging impacts that we are only starting to see. The sea level is rising as glaciers melt, which endangers the coastlines, affecting houses near the water and other ecosystems. The rising temperature of the ocean impacts the ecosystems that provide the seafood we consume. Companies that can help deal with this will create tremendous value.

5. **Cloud computing** - Cloud computing is the outsourcing of processing power and storage memory to computers stored elsewhere (off-premise) and then beamed back to you via a super-fast internet connection. Companies like Amazon Web Services (AWS), Microsoft's Azure, Salesforce, and Google Cloud now offer these services. Cloud computing helps companies adjust their computing (processing and memory) capacity as needed without investing in lots of hardware. They are renting the servers, instead of buying them.

6. **Artificial Intelligence (AI)** - Artificial intelligence refers to a computer's ability to increasingly predict outcomes that come close to mimicking the complexity of the human mind. With the gains in processing power and availability of data, computers can be programmed to predict, or think, as humans do. The human brain is so powerful that we can process things like an image of a car or various things on the road with some training (I got my driver's license at 16). Computers are not yet there, but many believe they will be one day. Currently, AI is all around us. AI is used by Facebook to predict the ads that you and I will likely click on. AI is used by Netflix to recommend shows based on your watching habits, and if you like that, it will recommend that show to people like you (who match your profile). It uses AI to decide what new shows to bankroll and develop. A major effort is underway to use AI to develop self-driving cars, which needs the computer (brains of the car) to process traffic lights, lanes, pedestrians, stop signs, other cars, lane closures, rain, snow, fog, bicycles, and animals crossing to get you safely from A to B. A self-driving car needs to process the world around it, calculate the best way to proceed, and drive you safely. The human brain can do it easily, but it is not yet easy for a computer to do that. AI will bring with it new and seemingly miraculous uses, and the companies that deliver that will earn a large amount of revenue and earnings. (Don't worry, we'll be sipping milkshakes in the Unicorn car soon enough)

7. **Electric vehicles (EV)** - This is a major secular shift. The modern world as we know it runs on fossil fuel in the form of crude oil that is extracted from the earth, refined into gasoline, diesel, plastic, and

loads of other useful things to power our cars, home, trucks, and make modern life possible. Electric vehicles instead will run on batteries charged overnight by electricity, negating our need for fossil fuels from America, the Middle East, and around the world. More importantly, we will not be releasing CO_2 into the ozone when we drive our EVs. CO_2 gets trapped in the atmosphere and warms the earth while smog pollutes the air in the cities we live in, contributing to health complications. Backing this trend is government policy in the U.S., Europe, and China. In 2021, the Biden Administration in the U.S. has goals of converting all government fleets into electric vehicles. In China, pollution is a big concern and the government has crafted policies to help the electric vehicle market thrive by supporting Chinese carmakers and giving discounts on electric car sales.

8. **Demographics** – The rise of the middle class in China, India, and emerging markets in Latin America and Southeast Asia have broad implications for the world as their views, demands, and consumption impact the world. The aging population in Japan, Europe, and the U.S. will also have broad implications for the economy and the market. Can you think of any industries, products, or goods that will need the needs of the changing demographics in your country/region?

9. **Esports and gaming** - Gaming in the U.S. brings in more revenues than movie and music sales combined. Gaming includes console games, PC games, and the fast-rising mobile games available on our smartphones and tablets. This popular form of entertainment is capturing an increasing amount of users' free time. The rise of esports, which is competitive video gaming, has captured attention

as it grows itself into a form of entertainment. Around the world, more and more people are watching other people play popular video games, compete, and win prizes. Recently, the winner of a Fortnite tournament won $3 million. Remember when your parents said playing video games would get you nowhere? Well, there are now competitive leagues and brand sponsorship for the best gamers. With the new consoles from Sony and Microsoft, a new generation will discover video games. In the past only your neighbors could come by the house to watch you play a game; now the whole world can sit next to you as you game.

10. **Gene editing** - Gene editing promises to solve illness and disease by fixing the very source of it in our genes. Our DNA is our individual blueprint for illness, disease, and other ailments. Though still in the initial stages of research, gene editing promises to find the malignancy in the blueprint and delete it, solving the problem of our body creating that very ailment. The human genome has been mapped and successful gene editing can potentially save a person from years of pain, financial stress from health bills, and eliminate unknown amounts of suffering. As you can imagine, the capital needs for research are high, but the potential revenues would be much greater.

Thought exercise: What are some other secular trends that you have observed?

Images: Illustrations throughout the chapter were sourced from Flaticon

CHAPTER 18

Risks

While evaluating an IPO, you must pay attention to a myriad of risks that can negatively impact your company and the industry it's in. In the S-, risks related to the business are spelled out in great detail in the "Risk Factors" section of the filing. No company is perfect, so knowing the risk and understanding how management plans to deal with it should give you confidence in the company as an investment.

Diving right in, let's take a look at peer-to-peer accommodations booking company Airbnb's risks. The company used the traditional IPO route to go public amidst a global travel ban as governments struggle to deal with the Covid-19 pandemic.

Exhibit 24 - Risk Factors from Airbnb's S-1

Risks Related to Our Business

The COVID-19 pandemic and the impact of actions to mitigate the COVID-19 pandemic have materially adversely impacted and will continue to materially adversely impact our business, results of operations, and financial condition.

In March 2020, the World Health Organization declared the outbreak of COVID-19 a pandemic. In an attempt to limit the spread of the virus, governments have imposed various restrictions, including emergency declarations at the federal, state, and local levels, school and business closings, quarantines, "shelter at home" orders, restrictions on travel, limitations on social or public gatherings, and other social distancing measures, which have had and may continue to have a material adverse impact on our business and operations and on travel behavior and demand.

The COVID-19 pandemic, which has required and may continue to require cost reduction measures, has materially adversely affected our near-term operating and financial results and will continue to materially adversely impact our long-term operating and financial results. During the fourth quarter of 2020, another wave of COVID-19 infections emerged. As a result, countries imposed strict lockdowns, in particular in Europe. Similar to the impact of the initial COVID-19 wave in March 2020, we are seeing a decrease in bookings in the most affected regions. As a result, we expect significantly greater year-over-year decline in Nights and Experiences Booked and GBV in the fourth quarter of 2020 than in the third quarter of 2020 and greater year-over-year increases in cancellations and alterations in the fourth quarter of 2020 than in the third quarter of 2020. In light of the evolving nature of COVID-19 and the uncertainty it has produced around the world, we do not believe it is possible to predict the COVID-19 pandemic's cumulative and ultimate impact on our future business, results of operations, and financial condition. The extent of the impact of the COVID-19 pandemic on our business and financial results will depend largely on future developments, including the duration and extent of the spread of COVID-19 both globally and within the United States, the prevalence of local, national, and international travel restrictions, significantly reduced flight volume, the impact on capital and financial markets and on the U.S. and global economies, foreign currencies exchange, and governmental or regulatory orders that impact our business, all of which are highly uncertain and cannot be predicted. Moreover, even after shelter-in-place orders and travel advisories are lifted, demand for our offerings, particularly those related to cross-border travel, may remain depressed for a significant length of time, and we cannot predict if and when demand will return to pre-COVID-19 levels. In addition, we cannot predict the impact the COVID-19 pandemic has had and will have on our business partners and third-party vendors and service providers, and we may continue to be materially adversely impacted as a result of the material adverse impact our business partners and third-party vendors suffer now and in the future. To the extent the COVID-19 pandemic continues to materially adversely affect our business, results of operations, and financial condition, it may also have the effect of heightening many

Certain Relationships and Related Party Transactions

In addition to the Risk Factors section of the S-1, the "Certain Relationships and Related Party Transactions" section could alert you to potential risks to account for. This section is where executives and board members disclose their acquisition of shares of the company, through limited liability corporations (LLCs) and other investment vehicles, before the IPO. We want to make sure that no major business is conducted by the company and another company owned by anyone high up in the company.

An infamous example is the WeWork IPO, which was derailed because it was disclosed in the S-1 that WE Holdings LLC (owned by CEO Adam Neumann) sold the rights to the "We Company" trademark to the company for $5.9 million in stock options. This is the statement from the "Equity Awards" subsection:

Exhibit 25 - WE Holdings Equity Awards

> In July 2019, WE Holdings LLC assigned residual rights related to "we" family trademarks to the Company, which we desired to obtain following our rebranding in early 2019. In consideration of this contribution and in lieu of paying cash, the Company issued to WE Holdings LLC partnership interests in the We Company Partnership with a fair market value of approximately $5.9 million, which was determined pursuant to a third-party appraisal.

CEO Adam Neumann also received a personal loan from the company.

Exhibit 26 - WE Holding's Personal Loan Disclosure

> **Company Loans**
>
> As a private company, in order to ensure alignment with our investor base, we have kept a captive capitalization table and have not allowed sales of equity other than in a manner organized by the Company. From time to time over the past several years, we made loans directly to Adam or his affiliated entities (in addition to the 2019 loan described above). None of these loans are outstanding as of the date of this prospectus.
>
> - In May 2013 and February 2014, we issued loans to WE Holdings LLC for $10.4 million (interest rate 0.2% per year; maturity May 30, 2016) and $15.0 million (interest rate 0.2% per year; maturity February 4, 2017), respectively. The loans were collateralized by shares of our capital stock held by We Holdings LLC, and each loan provided us with the option to purchase a number of these shares in full settlement of the applicable loan. We exercised these options in May 2016, purchasing and retiring an aggregate of 8,398,670 shares of our capital stock in full settlement of the loans.
> - In June 2016, we issued a loan to Adam totaling $7.0 million (interest rate of 0.64% per year; maturity June 14, 2019). In November 2017, Adam repaid the loan in full, including $0.1 million in interest, in cash.

Basically, the CEO paid himself from the company's coffers for the word "We" and then gave himself a low-cost loan, also from the company's coffers.

This is obviously a case of the CEO taking advantage of his position to enrich himself by selling a trademark at inflated prices and issuing a personal loan from the company's balance sheet to himself, to the detriment of the company. After this was disclosed, the CEO was forced to step down and the IPO was canceled. While this is an extreme example and won't happen very often, issues like this to a smaller degree do occur and thus, this section is very important to review as part of the IPO analysis process.

Moving beyond fraud and unscrupulous/illegal transactions, here are some of the top risks to look for when doing your due diligence research:

Competition

Is the company the very best in their market, the second best, or a fish in the sea with millions of other fish? I look for companies that do well and provide the best or better product or service vis-a-vis their competitors. If the company has a lot of competition, you will need to evaluate if they are at the top or at the bottom in terms of quality. We want to invest in companies that produce amazing products and services.

Low Profit Margins

Be careful of companies with low profit margins. This means they have a lot of competition, their products are not unique, there are lots of substitutes, and the company lacks brand loyalty so consumers will switch between the cheapest available products. Some industries with this trait include commodities, consumer staples, clothing, automobiles, etc. where many brands are competing. Within these highly competitive spaces, some companies can carve out a premium product and demand higher prices, like Nike within the apparel and footwear sector.

Nike has high profit margins because their products are associated with athletic excellence, the ability to perform and the spirit of pushing yourself to "just do it" ingrained into our minds through decades and millions of dollars of marketing. On the other side, restaurants are companies with low profit margins. Restaurants have high labor and food costs and end up making around 3% profits on food sold. In fact, most restaurants make a majority of their profits selling wine, beer, and cocktails where they can earn a high profit margin ($10 for a Corona at a restaurant when you can get a six-pack at a grocery store for $9.99). The restaurant business has low profit margins and depends on something that isn't its core offering, alcohol, to generate profits.

Lack of Brand Loyalty

A successful company will have repeat customers. These customers are willing to pay a premium price for the product relative to another brand offering a similar item. Nike, Louis Vuitton, Tesla, and Apple are brands that customers associate with excellent quality and thus will repeatedly buy their products. In exchange, these companies can charge higher prices. We will dig more into brand equity and brand loyalty in Chapter 22.

Key Man Risk

While it has been in vogue to invest in a company with a well-known and beloved founder/CEO leading the company, this actually has a lot of risks. What if that person leaves, misbehaves, or commits a crime? Once they are gone, will the company implode? If the company's cultures and systems cannot survive and thrive without the CEO at the helm, then there is significant key man risk. You must look for a company that has a well-balanced team of leaders and a strong culture that can thrive when stars leave the company. The company must have a deep bench, to use a football analogy, where talent is abundant.

Some of the most famous companies have key man risks, as their corporate identity and culture are associated with one person. Some examples include Jeff Bezos of Amazon, Mark Zuckerberg of Facebook, and Elon Musk of Tesla. These CEOs and their personalities define the company to consumers, investors, suppliers, and politicians more than their employees do. They represent a cult of personality where the founder/CEO represents what the company stands for. Without them, it could be perceived that the company might lose its way by not investing in the right initiatives or losing its innovative edge.

How do you counter or at least account for key man risk? Try to understand if the company has a strong enough corporate culture to survive without the CEO. Said differently, does the CEO define the company's culture, or is actually the company culture that emanates onto its employees and the CEO just happens to represent that ethos really well? We'll discuss this in more depth in Chapter 19.

Chinese Variable Interest Entity (VIE) Structure

Chinese companies have chosen to go public in the U.S. to access America's wealth and more mature stock market to raise capital. Oftentimes, household names in China are virtually unknown in the United States, but the Chinese companies still find it easier to raise money in the U.S. due to the sheer assets managed by funds that operate in the world's largest stock market. You might run into a few companies from China looking to list their shares. One risk is the Variable Interest Entity structure, or VIE, used by some companies. China bans foreigners from owning sensitive Chinese companies. Investment bankers came up with the VIE structure, which creates a shell company in the Cayman Islands that has contracts with the Chinese company to operate, manage, and receive profits from that company. In theory, the shell company runs the operations of and receives all profits from the real company, and then distributes it to its shareholders.

As an American investor in companies like Alibaba, the e-commerce and clouding computing giant founded by Jack Ma, you don't actually own Alibaba; China wouldn't allow it. You own a Cayman Island company that has contracts to operate Alibaba and receive Alibaba's profits. This has been standard practice on Wall Street, but legal scholars believe if China one day wanted to rule the VIE structure as illegal, American investors would have no recourse. In such a case, the Cayman Island company owned by American investors would have no legal claim to the Chinese company because its contracts would be ruled illegal and voided. This is a significant risk that you should be aware of when analyzing IPOs of Chinese companies, considering both the shaky legal framework of the VIE structure and the rising tensions between the U.S. and China as economic rivals.

These are some of the big risks to look for but it's not a comprehensive list as each industry and each company will have its own unique set of challenges and risks.

Thought exercise: Take a company, any company that you might buy from or love, and list out three risks to their business.

CHAPTER 19

Corporate Culture

As we discussed in the last chapter, Key Man Risk can be mitigated by a strong corporate culture that doesn't chain its identity to a founder/CEO. So how do you know a good corporate culture from a bad one? Here are some key elements to look for and how you can spot them:

Good Management Team

Companies that have stood the test of time, through decades and different generations, have a strong corporate culture that focuses on innovation, investing for the long term, and are "customer focused" by striving to serve the customer's every need, present and anticipated, as they evolve over time. You can learn more about the current executives running the company in the "Management" section of the S-1. It will contain a list of all the executive officers and directors, as well as their biographies and work history. Learning about the management team can give you confidence in their experience and work history and what they might bring from working at other great companies.

Innovative Mindset

Search for sections "Business" and "Use of Proceeds" in the S-1 filing to find potential uses of the money raised, including technological investments or lists of new products in the works by the company. The company's mission statement could also reveal its long-term goals. Lastly, the company should demonstrate the ability to create innovative and new products. Apple, under Steve Jobs, launched the iPod, iPhone, iPad, Apple TV, and iMac. Steve Jobs was a big influence on the trajectory of the company, but the company's culture also enforced the innovative DNA that pushed it to iterate and innovate on new and better, faster and bigger, versions of their products to the customer's delight.

Learning About a Company's Culture

The first stop should be the company's website, either in the Careers section or in the About Us section. The descriptions you will find here are positive and often marketing fluff designed to make the company look great. Within the S-1, you can read about culture in the "Prospectus Summary" and in the founder/CEO letter in the "Business" section, as well as the company's mission statement.

But where do you go to hear employees talk about corporate culture? On websites like Glassdoor, employees post reviews of what it is like to work for the company. Also, check on Yelp and Google Reviews for customer reviews. Lastly, if it's a product, look at consumer review websites (*Car and Driver*, Cnet, TrustPilot, etc.) or scan for headlines in major newspapers to understand public sentiment towards new products and services.

What the employee has to say about the company and what customers say about the company will reveal how strong the corporate culture is. Happy employees strive to make their companies great and happy customers remain loyal and offer a lifetime of repeat business. Corporate culture rankings and lists like IBD's Top 50 Most Innovative, or Deloitte's Technology Fast 500 list are great sources to see the industries and companies that are innovative. Another great source is the various "Best Places to Work" awards, which will give you a feel for how the company treats its employees. Happy employees can mean low turnover, high productivity, and a competitive edge because you are not losing employees to rivals.

Customer Focused

Look for companies that are rigorously focused on satisfying their customer's needs, both present needs and those they anticipate in the future. A great example of this is Starbucks, which implemented a loyalty program to reward its customers with free drinks and treats, pushed into digital payments and mobile ordering to make the ordering process quicker, and gathered data about its customers to better serve them. When you delight your customers, they will come back and pay a premium for that experience.

Long-term Focused

You've heard that companies who invest for the long term tend to win versus short-term oriented firms who are caught off guard by secular changes. It's rare to see a long term focus in companies and rarer for public companies because of Wall Street's pressure to deliver quarterly results that beat Wall Street analyst expectations. The majority of public companies focus on delivery revenue and earnings (profits) that beat those analyst estimates. This often requires lower costs for marketing, sales, research and development (R&D), to focus on increasing profit margins, both gross and net. Without R&D investments, companies will be without innovative products and services to launch in the future and ultimately lose market share to firms with newer and advanced products. Again, S-1 filing sections "Business" and "Use of Proceeds" are good places to start looking.

Amazon, the dominant e-commerce retailer and cloud computing giant, is known to be very long-term focused; often sacrificing profits by immediately reinvesting revenue in new areas of service. Amazon's successful e-commerce business bankrolled the rise of Amazon Web Services (AWS), its more profitable cloud computing business after it realized it could rent excess computing power by letting companies run programs "in the cloud" on Amazon's extra servers. It then used the profits from the AWS business to build out features of the e-commerce business including Amazon Prime delivery in addition to completely new business lines such as Amazon Studios, the Echo digital assistant speaker, Fire TV dongles, and to acquire Whole Foods to be more competitive in online grocery deliveries. Through it all, they have used proceeds from profitable segments of their business to invest in new, riskier, innovative, and customer focused areas. There are times when they fail—like with the Fire Phone which was a flop and with their Food Delivery Business which they shut down—but by investing for and focusing on the long term, they have been able to deliver great products and services ahead of anyone else.

Buying $1,000 of Amazon (AMZN) stock on the day of its IPO, May 17, 1997, would lead to a cumulative return of 166,155%, or an annualized return of 37%, turning that initial $1,000 investment into $1,622,547 as of December 31, 2020.

Thought exercise: From your own experience, what company do your friends speak proudly about working for and what companies do people dread?

CHAPTER 20

Valuation

There is one major distinction and talking point that will be very important to focus on when a company goes public: is it profitable yet or not? Profits are also known as "earnings" or formally as "net income" from the income statement. We're going to dive into company valuation, with an overview of the basic valuation ratios and a discussion of what is appropriate to use for companies making profits and companies that are not yet profitable. Within the S-1, the Selected Consolidated Financial and Other Data section is where you will find important financial statements along with company specific metrics such as users and average revenue per customer. For comparison purposes, we'll look at companies that are already trading publicly. Their earnings and revenue data can be found in the company's 10-Q quarterly filing or 10-K annual filing available on the SEC's www.sec.gov/EDGAR website.

Before we get into a discussion on what valuation methods to use, let's go over the basics. After the basics, let's apply that valuation method to the e-commerce example we touched on in Chapter 17 to bring things full circle.

Market Capitalization (Valuation)

Market Capitalization, or "Market Cap" for short, refers to the total value of the company as determined by the current share price times the total number of outstanding shares. It is also sometimes referred to as the "valuation" of the company. One fun way to remember this concept is the market cap is how much you (or another company) will have to pay to buy the entire company.

Market Cap = Current Share Price x Total Outstanding Shares

For example, if a stock is trading at $15 per share and the total shares outstanding is 100 million, then the company's market cap = $15 x 100,000,000 or $1,500,000,000 or $1.5 billion. Companies with a market cap below $2 billion are usually considered small companies (small caps) and those with market caps between $2–$5 billion are considered medium companies (mid caps) and any company with a market cap above $5 billion is considered large (large cap).

Recall in Chapter 17's discussion of secular trends, we talked about the regional leaders of E-commerce around the world. Here is a look at their respective market capitalizations.

Exhibit 27 - E-Commerce Market Caps

Image: Designed with resources from Flaticon
Source: Factset

Earnings Per Share (EPS)

Earnings Per Share or "EPS" refers to the earnings, or profits, earned each year divided by the total shares of the company. It is simply how much profit (earnings) your share of the company (stock) generated in a year.

EPS = Net Income / Total Shares Outstanding

This can be thought of as the profits per share generated by the company and is a useful metric for analyzing profitability between two or more companies across different sectors, industries, etc. While a stockholder will not keep all of those earnings, as companies can choose to pay dividends or reinvest in the earnings, the EPS does represent the profits the company can earn from its business operations.

Let's go over some of the most common valuation metrics and the underlying reasons why they are used to justify a stock price or what someone thinks a stock price should be.

Price to Earnings (P/E)

Let's put it all together to calculate the Price to Earnings (P/E) ratio:

P/E = Market Cap/Net Income

Or

P/E = Share Price/Earnings Per Share

You might have noticed the second formula is really just the first formula's components divided by the total shares. So just to be clear, this is what I mean:

P/E = (Market Cap/Total Shares) / (Net Income/Total Shares)

The Price to Earnings (P/E) Ratio is how much you pay for $1 of profit generated by that business each year. Price is the stock price of a single share, and Earnings is the 12-month Earnings Per Share (EPS). Historically, the S&P 500 index has had an average P/E ratio of 18. This is referred to as the "market multiple" since the biggest 500 companies in the U.S. make up the majority of the publicly traded stock market. Another way to think about this is: for the right to a business's $1 of annual profits forever, you are willing to pay $18 today. Using finance lingo, you are willing to pay 18 times the amount of annual profits, so the P/E ratio is often expressed with an "x" to indicate it is 18 times profit, so a P/E = 18x. The Price to Earnings ratio is a helpful valuation metric to use because you can compare the value of different businesses on a common denominator: $1 of profit. A company is considered more expensive if it trades at a higher P/E multiple because you are paying more for $1 of profits.

When buying and selling homes, you often look at what other homes in the neighborhood sell for. You look for similar homes, with the same number of bedrooms and bathrooms and square footage and use those as your list of comparisons. Agents and buyers often refer to the Price Per Square Foot of a house as a quick comparison. A house selling for $300 per square foot is more expensive than a house selling for $250 per square foot. The $300 house might be newer, with updated kitchens and floors, or a more desirable modern design, or in a better neighborhood with coffee shops, parks, and good schools, thus justifying a higher price.

Using that analogy, let's think about why someone would pay more for $1 of future profits. Isn't it the same $1, regardless of where it comes from? Well, simply put, some companies are better and more desirable than others. A company with a P/E ratio of 25 might be the leader in their industry, they might be known to have loyal customers and well-regarded products, they might have a higher profit margin which means it takes less revenue to earn that $1 of profit, or they might be in a sector that isn't heavily regulated. Overall, their business model, product, management team, or industry might simply have better prospects. Healthy food companies might have a higher P/E versus fast food as investors see a secular trend toward healthy eating. Electric vehicle companies might command a higher P/E than gas powered automakers as electric vehicles become more desirable. Internet companies might have a higher P/E than print newspapers because internet companies require less infrastructure, have a larger customer base, and sell their ads every day to readers online while newspapers sell their ads to those that pick up a physical copy.

That was too theoretical, I thought we were going to use real-world examples? Show me how it works in the real world.

P/E in the Real World

Let's focus on the e-commerce space we began to explore in Chapter 17 and look at the P/E ratio of several e-commerce companies to see how they stack up against each other in what is called a peer comparables analysis ("peer comps"). To make it more robust, let's add two more e-commerce companies: eBay from the U.S. and JD.com from China. In a peer comps analysis, we compare companies that compete and have similar business models. E-commerce companies are marketplaces or platforms where a buyer and seller meet to transact. The e-commerce company charges a percentage of the transaction value called the "take rate" for providing the infrastructure (website, secure payments, fraud detection, authenticity check, and/or shipping) to make the transaction possible. To calculate the P/E, I retrieved the companies' 10-K financial statements from www.SEC.gov/edgar and divided the current stock price by the calendar year 2020 EPS, which covers the 1/1/2020 – 12/31/2020 period. Here is how they stack up.

Exhibit 28 - Price to Earnings (P/E) Ratio

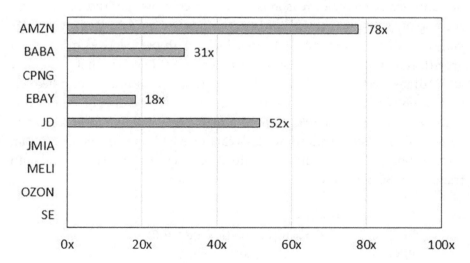

The P/E ranges from 18x to 78x. Amazon has the highest P/E ratio, while eBay has the lowest. Five companies don't have a P/E because they don't have positive earnings yet. This is also referred to as having negative earnings, operating at a loss, or just plain unprofitable. We can't compare those companies using P/E because negative earnings would calculate a negative P/E ratio which we can't use, demonstrating the limitations of this method. Let's work with what we have, which is the 4 companies with positive earnings. A higher P/E indicates the market believes that $1 of earnings is of higher quality (perhaps they believe this e-commerce platform is much more popular and durable while the other one isn't meeting customers' needs) and thus more likely to grow and take market share in the future.

In layman's terms, a company which you expect to be more profitable in the future should garner a higher P/E ratio today. The house on a quiet street will be sold for more than the same exact house near a busy freeway because it is more desirable. Given the option of two comparable e-commerce companies, if you expect one to be more profitable next year, you would pay a little more to own that one today. How do you quantify that expectation?

Price to Earnings Growth Ratio (PEG)

There are many reasons why companies' P/E ratios might be different from one another, but a major reason is the expected growth of future earnings. A company with great growth prospects might see its earnings grow by 25% next year while a company with inferior growth perspectives might see a growth rate of 0%. Let's use shoes as an example. Let's say that both Nike and Adidas trade at a P/E ratio of 18x. Adidas then announces a big collaboration with a hip-hop artist to exclusively carry her line of shoes while Nike will only grow at 10% without a major new collaboration to match. As a result, investors believe Adidas's earnings will grow by 25% next year. Assume both Nike and Adidas had $10 of earnings per share (EPS) and both traded at $180 per share.

$$P/E = 180 / 10 = 18x$$
$$PEG = (P/E) / (\text{Earnings Growth Rate} * 100)$$
$$PEG \text{ (Nike)} = 18 / (0.10 \times 100) = 1.80$$
$$PEG \text{ (Adidas)} = 18 / (0.25 \times 100) = 0.72$$

At $180 current shares and $10 current earnings, both stocks seem to be similar and fairly valued without any differentiation. But, given the announcement of the collaboration, Adidas stock seems to have better prospects with a 25% growth rate next year vs Nike's 10%. While these earnings are in the future and haven't been realized yet, we can compare the expected growth and see that Adidas with a 25% growth is cheaper than Nike, based on the PEG comparison of 0.72 vs 1.80. $1 of future Adidas earnings will be cheaper than $1 of Nike earnings because it will grow faster. Said another way, 1 share of Adidas will get you $12.50 of earnings next year while 1 share of Nike will only get you $11.00 of earnings.

> $10 growing 10% is $11.00
> $10 growing 25% is $12.50

The PEG ratio was popularized by Peter Lynch, the famous portfolio manager of the Fidelity Magellan Fund. He used the PEG ratio to address the shortcomings of the P/E ratio by factoring in projected growth rates of future earnings. He believed a PEG of 1 means the stock is fairly priced, a PEG less than 1 means the stock is undervalued and considered a good buy, and a PEG greater than 1 is considered overvalued. Therefore, Adidas stock is the better value with a PEG of 0.72 compared to Nike stock's PEG of 1.80 because it is expected to earn more profits in the future despite the same share price and earnings today.

PEG in the Real World

Let's compare our e-commerce companies using PEG. The P/E calculations are the same, but I will use the 2019–2020 earnings growth rate as the denominator. A 1-year growth rate is a simple and quick calculation, but in practice, a trailing 3-year or 5-year annualized growth rate might be used by wall street to predict the future earnings of companies.

Here is what that PEG peer comps table looks like.

Exhibit 29 - Price to Earnings Growth (PEG) Ratio

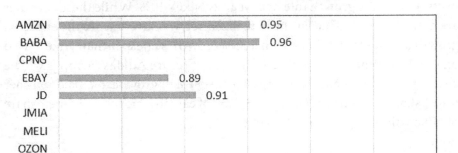

What sticks out immediately? The PEG ratios are between 0.89 and 0.96 which is a very tight range and there is virtually no dispersion like what we saw with the P/E ratio. The PEG comparison is telling us that these 4 companies are very fairly priced relative to how fast they are growing earnings. While we saw a large variation in the P/E, the PEG is telling us that the P/E dispersion is justified because the future of each e-commerce platform is different: some have better earnings prospects and deserve a higher P/E. Those growth prospects are weighted using the PEG.

While that gives us a better understanding of the 4 companies with positive earnings (profitable), what about the 5 companies that aren't yet profitable and have negative earnings? The math doesn't work out for them, but surely, they have some value?

Price to Sales Ratio (P/S)

Let's look at their revenues ("sales" is used interchangeably with revenues) to try to value the company based on how much product or services it can sell to customers. This multiple is used for companies that do not yet have profits (earnings) and are still operating at a loss. They are in the early stages of growth and have come to the public market to sell their shares in the IPO to raise cash for more growth. If they don't have earnings, you can't use the P/E or the PEG ratios to compare. What you can do is use the crude and rudimentary, but simple, Price to Sales (P/S) ratio which compares two companies based on their revenues or sales. While we want to own a stock for its future profits, since the company is so young, we will have to take a leap of faith and assume it can earn similar profit margins to mature peers in the distant future on those sales.

Here is the formula:

Price to Sales Ratio = Price Per Share / Revenue Per Share

Or

Price to Sales Ratio = Market Cap / Annual Revenue

Or

Price to Sales Ratio = Price Per Share / (Annual Revenue/Total Share Count)

P/S in the Real World

Okay, so you might have noticed that the five companies including Coupang, Ozon, Jumia, Mercado Libre, and Sea Limited have no earnings yet, so the P/E and its derivative, the PEG are useless. These are younger companies, and might be profitable one day, but aren't yet. It doesn't mean they are worth nothing. To assign a value to companies that aren't profitable yet, we look to their sales and use the Price to Sales (P/S) ratio (remember, Sales = Revenues). Here, we measure how much money we are paying for $1 of the company's sales each year. To get P/S, I divide the current share price by the full year 2020 revenues as found in the company's 10-Q or 10-K filing.

This is what the P/S ratio of all nine E-commerce companies look like:

Exhibit 30 - Price to Sales (P/S) Ratio

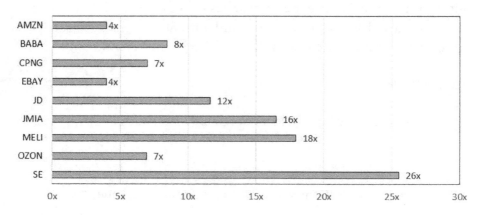

For the first time, we get to see how the five unprofitable companies (CPNG, OZON, JMIA, MELI, SE) stack up against each other and the four profitable companies (AMZN, EBAY, BABA, JD). SE has the most expensive valuation, followed by MELI and JMIA. AMZN and EBAY have the lowest P/S valuations.

Shockingly, Amazon (AMZN) has the highest P/E at 78x, a reasonable PEG of 0.95, and the lowest P/S at 4x. P/S allows us to compare all the companies on an apples-to-apples basis. Amazon, with its long operating history and larger market U.S. customer base, has much more in revenues than the other companies. The wide dispersion in the P/S tells us that the market has very different expectations of sales growth. So how do we improve on the P/S? You guessed it: by incorporating the growth rate of sales just like we incorporated the growth rate of earnings to get the PEG.

Price to Sales Growth (PSG)

To get PSG, I need to calculate sales (revenue) growth from 2019 to 2020. Once I have that growth rate, I take the P/S ratio and divided it by the Sales Growth rate to get the table below. Here is the formula, the first with ratios and the second breaking down the underlying calculations.

PSG = (Price/Sales) / (Sales Growth)
PSG = (Market Cap/2020 Revenue) / (2020 Revenue/2019 Revenue)

Exhibit 31 - Price to Sales Growth (PSG) Ratio

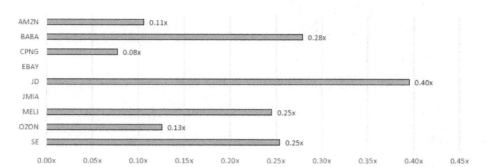

What are we looking at when we look at PSG? We are looking at how much money we pay for $1 of sales, given the growth rate of sales. The lower the ratio, the better. Just like a lower P/S means we pay less money for $1 of sales, a lower PSG ratio means we pay less money for $1 of sales growth. Amazon continues to stack up well, but CPNG has the lowest PSG ratio. JD, the Chinese E-commerce firm has the highest PSG, which means we are paying the most money for $1 of sales growth or almost 4 times as much for $1 of sales growth from Amazon (0.40x for JD vs 0.11x for AMZN). You'll notice EBAY and JMIA are off the board, as they experienced a sales decline. Mathematically, they don't generate a PSG but intuitively, we do not want to invest in a company that is seeing sales decline.

Calculations

On the next page in Table 10 are the numbers from our companies' 10-K and 10-Q filings and the simple formulas used to calculate P/E, PEG, P/S, and PSG. I didn't want to clog up our discussion with a big chart so I saved it for last. Also, please note the averages of the growth rates and the 4 ratios discussed.

Table 10 – Valuation Calculations

Ticker	Price	Total Shares (m)	Market Cap ($ m)	2020 Revenue ($ m)	2019 Revenue ($ m)	2020 EPS	2019 EPS	EPS Growth =(2020 EPS/2019 EPS)-1	Sale Growth =(2020 Rev/2019 Rev)-1	P/E =(Price/2020 EPS)	PEG =(P/E)/(EPS Growth*100)	P/S =(Market Cap/2020 Revenue)	PSG =(P/S)/Sales Growth*100
AMZN	3,257	472	1,538,500	386,100	280,500	41.83	23.01	82%	38%	78x	0.95	4x	0.11
EBAY	62	662	41,044	10,271	10,719	3.41	2.83	20%	-4%	18x	0.89	4x	N/A
BABA	233	2,653	618,100	73,163	56,149	7.42	5.59	33%	30%	31x	0.96	8x	0.28
JD	84	14,952	1,256,000	108,052	83,488	1.63	1.04	57%	29%	52x	0.91	12x	0.40
SE	199	560	111,400	4,365	2,178	(2.78)	(2.00)	N/A	100%	N/A	N/A	26x	0.25
MELI	1,675	43	71,215	3,973	2,296	(0.08)	(3.71)	N/A	73%	N/A	N/A	18x	0.25
JMIA	33	84	2,786	169	180	(2.39)	(3.14)	N/A	-6%	N/A	N/A	16x	N/A
OZON	56	179	10,014	1,442	929	N/A	(1.42)	N/A	55%	N/A	N/A	7x	0.13
CPNG	49	1,708	83,672	11,967	6,273	N/A	(0.48)	N/A	91%	N/A	N/A	7x	0.08
Average								48%	45%	45x	0.93	11x	0.21

You might be thinking: But Nam, this looks like a lot of work. I need to dig around the S-1 and then I need to find similar companies…and then I need to track down their financial data?

Yup. But a quicker way to get all of this data is through Yahoo! Finance, which allows you to search for these figures in an easy-to-use interface.

What's the Ideal Valuation?

Question: What's the ideal valuation?

Answer: Below or near the peer group average.

Whether you are using P/E, PEG, P/S, or PSG, if the valuation is close to the average or below it, great. Valuation is very difficult at the IPO stage because the company is young, it is asking for more money to grow and usually hasn't earned a profit yet (no earnings, net income negative). The future of the company is very uncertain, with profits years away and likely competition from new and old companies alike. If the P/S and P/E ratios are close to incumbent public firms, then it could be a great deal. More often than not, the P/S and P/E are much higher than incumbents because the expectation for growth is baked in. Every sector and company will come with different valuation challenges but as long as the P/S or P/E is not too much higher than a group of similar companies and the company has the characteristics outlined in the other Tool Kit sections, it could make for a good investment. Companies with profits and thus a P/E ratio that can be calculated are relatively safer and easier to analyze than companies without profits because with a P/S analysis alone, there is a chance that the company will never be profitable and never reach that stage in its life where revenues will outpace expenses. While the ideal valuation would be below or near the peer group, you'll often find great and enduring businesses have high valuations that are above their peer averages. Companies with above-average valuations need to have a majority of the thirteen characteristics to justify their relatively more expensive shares.

Discussion of Valuation

Typical valuation methods like Price to Earnings won't apply to a company going public because they are often "pre-profit" or not yet profitable.

Wait...shouldn't a company be mature and profitable by the time they are ready to go public in an IPO? In the past, companies have waited to become profitable before selling their shares to the public, but in the past two decades that has changed. With the rise of internet and technology companies in the 1990s, companies are now going public because they need more capital to grow despite being years away from profitability. Younger companies invest a lot in research, capital equipment, factories, and marketing (discounts) to win customers and raise revenue. In the early stage of a company's life, its goal is to grow sales and win customers. This strategy is used to win market share early and gain customer loyalty. Some examples include JetBlue offering $60 flights from New York to Miami. Uber offering the first ride free, or Square giving away $20 to download and use its Cash app. As those investments are made and a customer base is created, the promotions slow down. As expenses slow and revenues continue to grow, net income becomes positive. This is called "operating leverage" as the company keeps its cost growth slower than revenue growth.

A classic example is the lemonade stand, which requires upfront investments of a table, lemon, water, sugar, a pitcher, cups, and ice along with signs for marketing to neighbors. As kids make lemonade sales throughout the day, the revenue grows and eventually covers the fixed cost of the lemonade stand.

Companies rarely go public when they are mature and realizing profits. Instead, they go public when they need more money because the IPO allows them to sell their equity to investors in exchange for money, to invest and grow their business with the plan that profits come down the line (years or decades later).

Deeper Dive into Valuation Methods

Valuation is a very complex topic and there have been numerous books written to cover methods including the discounted cash flow model (DCF), the Sum-of-the-Parts method (SOTP), and a plethora of different ratios. I recommend watching valuation videos from New York University's Aswath Damodaran on YouTube or on his NYU website, which can be found with a quick internet search. He is a superstar in the finance world and does an excellent job teaching valuation. Anything you can learn from his videos would complement what you have learned in this book in terms of using the IPO Tool Kit to find compelling IPOs to invest in for the long term.

CHAPTER 21

SPAC Valuation

SPACs, the focus of chapter 3, should be analyzed as IPOs using the same Tool Kit with a long-term investment horizon. Investing in stock via IPO, SPAC, or direct listing are all different ways of ultimately buying businesses and should be treated as such. However, the valuation of a SPAC requires a different method, so let's dive in.

Theory vs Reality

SPAC shares will be issued at $10 per share as mentioned in chapter 3. In theory, before a merger announcement is made, the shares should remain at $10 because no one knows what business they will merge with. However, shares often gain based on rumors or speculation of what private company the SPAC might merge with. Another theory posits that the $10 should be the absolute minimum because the SPAC allows you to redeem $10 per share if you do not like the merger announced. However, some SPACs have traded below $10 as the SPAC struggles to find a company to merge within the allotted two years before they are required to return investor money. This is due to investors losing interest and choosing to take less than $10 per share to sell and use those proceeds to reinvest elsewhere.

For our purposes, we will focus on the SPAC after a formal merger announcement with a private company is made. Any price movements before that are a result of market speculation.

SPAC Merger Valuation

When a SPAC and a company determine they are a good match, the process of the merger starts. A big part of that process in addition to telling the story of the business is the valuation of the company. There's no maximum size of a target company, only a minimum size that is required equal to 80% of the funds in the SPAC trust.

Let's walk through a quick example of how to calculate the market cap of a SPAC after it merges with a company. As a refresher, the Market Cap = Total Shares Outstanding x Share Price. This is also considered the valuation of the company or the price of the company.

In our example, let's use a fictional SPAC by the name of Renewable Energy Management YieldCo with the ticker REMY. REMY stock currently trades at $10 per share and shareholders collectively have 40 million (m) shares, and they will own 20% of the post-merger company. Shares outstanding and post-merger ownership will be clearly spelled out in the SPAC "investor presentation" usually made available on their website and through SEC's Edgar filing.

REMY market cap = ($10 x 40 m shares) / 0.20 = $2.0 billion

Put another way, the REMY shares are worth 10 x 40 m = $400 million. Since REMY will own 20% of the company after the merger, you multiply the 20% portion times 5 to get to 100% (this is the same as dividing $400 m by 20%). Therefore, $400m x 5 = $2,000 m or $2.0 billion (b).

If the stock price of REMY increases to $20, then the market cap will be, assuming no additional shares are issued, $20 x 40 m / 0.20 = $4.0 b. The math checks out here: if you double the share price, you double the market cap.

Some warrants can be exercised after the merger if the price is above a threshold (e.g., $15). If warrants are exercised, then new shares are added to the equation and increase the market cap. For example, if 10 m shares are added by warrants being exercised, then the share count goes up to 50 m. If the share price stays the same, the new market cap is:

REMY's market cap post warrant exercise =
($10 x 50 m share) / 0.20 = $2.5 b

In real life, the new shares will often drive the stock price down while keeping the market capitalization the same. This is called share dilution as each share is effectively worth less because it owns a smaller fraction of the company.

Valuation with PIPE Financing

Recall our discussion of additional financing by way of a Private Investment in Public Equity (PIPE) financing. What does this look like exactly? Let's take a look at a recent SPAC named Churchill Capital IV (Ticker: CCIV) that announced it is merging with electric vehicle maker Lucid Motors in 2021 as an illustrative example.

In the S-4 form filed with the SEC, you can find the "Pro-Forma Ownership" table which lists how many shares are owned by whom. "Pro-forma" is finance jargon and just means forward-looking, referring to the period after the SPAC and the private company have successfully merged. They will offer two hypothetical tables, one assuming "no redemption" and the other assuming "maximum redemption". Recall, if holders of CCIV decide they don't like Lucid Motors as the acquisition target, they can redeem their stock for $10 per share. For simplicity's sake, let's assume shareholders like the acquisition and focus our analysis on the "no redemption" pro-forma table for this SPAC.

Table 11 – SPAC Merger Pro-Forma Ownership

	No. of Shares (Million)	% Shares Outstanding
Lucid Shareholders	1,177.02	73.5%
Churchill Sponsor ("Promote")	51.75	3.2%
Churchill Public Stockholders (CCIV)	207.00	12.9%
PIPE Investors	166.66	10.4%
Total Pro-Forma Shares Outstanding	**1,602.44**	**100.0%**

After the merger, existing Lucid Motors shareholders will own 73.5% of the company. The PIPE investors will own 10.4%, the CCIV shareholders will own 12.9% and the CCIV SPAC management team will be rewarded with a 3.2% ownership stake for their efforts in organizing the merger between CCIV and Lucid Motors.

Valuation (Calculating the Market Cap)

The PIPE deal raised $2,500 million for Lucid Motors, and they sold 10.4% of the company to institutional investors.

Thus, the PIPE valued Lucid Motors at a market cap of:

Market Cap = $2,500 million / 10.4% = 24,038 million or $24 billion.

We can also calculate what the PIPE investors paid per share by simple division:

Share Price = $2,500 million / 166.66 million shares = $15 per share

Recall in Chapter 3, we learned in theory the SPAC should trade at $10 per share before a formal announcement is made. However, in the real world, rumors and speculation move the price. In this real world example, Bloomberg news speculated that CCIV would acquire Lucid Motors in a published article titles "Lucid Motors Is Said to Near Deal to List Via Klein's SPAC". This caused the price to jump up as investors clamored for the next hot electric vehicle stock.

Continuing on our valuation example, let's use the real world SPAC (CCIV) price of $60 per share, which is the last closing price before the deal was formally announced on February 22, 2021, instead of the theoretical $10. That yields a much different valuation for Lucid Motors:

Market Cap = ($60 x 207.00 million shares) / 12.9% = 96,279 million
or $96.3 billion

The PIPE investors got a great deal, buying shares for $15 per share while the SPAC shares (CCIV) were trading in the public market for $60 due to speculation ahead of the deal announcement. They received a huge discount and this could be thought of as the IPO "pop" that is again reserved for the small group of institutional investors. The SPAC will usually trade at a higher market cap as the PIPE shares are sold at a discount (cheaper per share) to a small group of institutional investors as discussed in Chapter 3. However, the CCIV shares will continue to trade until the deal is completed. There exist two different market cap valuations driven by the PIPE deal and by the publicly traded shares under the ticker CCIV.

Table 12 – Two Valuations, One Company

	Share Price	Market Cap (Valuation)
Churchill Public Stockholders (CCIV)	$60	$96.3 billion
PIPE Investors	$15	$24.0 billion

So, what is the right valuation? Is it determined by the SPAC trading price or the PIPE deal valuation?

The answer is, somewhere in the middle. Until the deal is completed, the SPAC price is the most current valuation because it represents the only public shares available, and that valuation takes its cue from the PIPE valuation. In our case, after the PIPE deal was formally announced, CCIV shares lost nearly half of their value and traded down from $60 to $35 the next day. It traded down closer to the $15 per share PIPE price because the market views these institutional investors as being savvier and more sophisticated; trusting their PIPE valuation is probably closer to the real value of the company.

Using either the CCIV or PIPE market cap as a starting point, you now have a market cap number to use to perform the peer comparables ratio analysis discussed in Chapter 20 which includes P/E, PEG, P/S, and PSG. Using the PIPE market cap as a starting point can be viewed as a conservative approach because you are taking what the institutional investors paid as the basis for comparing it against other companies. Using the most recent

CCIV market cap, which depends on the current price of the CCIV shares multiplied by all shares outstanding, could be more relevant as it is the most recently quoted price for the stock.

Theory vs Reality, Revisited

This example presented a nice contrast between theory and reality. In theory, CCIV shares should have been around $10 until a formal merger announcement was made. In theory, CCIV should have traded up to $15, the same valuation the PIPE investors paid for their shares. This would've given the CCIV holders a 50% return ($5 per share gain). But in reality, speculation pushed the CCIV price all the way to $60 per share before any official announcement and when the PIPE deal was announced at $15 per share, prices of CCIV crashed and traded down closer to the $15 agreed upon by the PIPE investors.

Does Management Deserve the Promote?

In table 11, you've surely noticed that the management team of the SPAC will be rewarded with 51.75 million shares of Lucid Motors or 3.2% of the company after the merger (known as the "promote") for their role in setting up the SPAC and finding the acquisition. While the management team didn't earn a salary throughout the process of searching for an acquisition, the total value of the Churchill Sponsor "promote" payout is gargantuan. They will be awarded 51.75 million shares, which when valued at the conservative PIPE price of $15 per share is worth $776 million. That is a big payday for a management team and begs the question: Do their efforts and the ultimate outcome merit such a big financial payday?

Companies with No Revenues Are Speculative

Remember when we thought a company needed to be profitable to go public? Yes, investing in a company before profitability is risky. But, how about a company that does not have any revenue (sales) at all? Companies with no revenues ("pre-revenue" is the term to soften the negativity) do go public too, and more often now than ever. One such company is Lucid Motors, the valuation example we just worked through. They have yet to sell any cars when the SPAC merger with CCIV was announced. Therefore, they do not have any revenues or earnings for us to perform the traditional P/E, PEG, P/S, and PSG valuation ratio analysis.

In a recent article from Loup Ventures, which was founded by famed Apple analyst Gene Munster, titled "SPACs are Venture Capital in Public Market", the firm describes the trend of companies coming to the public market at a much younger stage in their lives for capital. SPAC is replacing the VC fundraising stages that take place before maturity and the subsequent IPO. SPACs are thought of as an alternative route to IPOs, but the companies they are going public are usually less mature than those that venture to the markets in the traditional IPO route. Some SPACs acquire companies with just an idea, that is, a product or service in development. The company doesn't have any revenue yet but perhaps does have a large partner or a committed list of buyers once the product is ready. These companies are called "Pre-Revenue" and usually do not hit the public markets so early, but through SPACs, they can. According to Loup Ventures, SPACs are the democratization of venture capital, as regular investors can buy these companies at a much earlier stage in their life that is usually reserved for venture capital funds such as Sequoia and Andreessen Horowitz.

SPACs without revenues are speculative. It's not to say they will fail or will never generate revenue in the future, but without a solid history of performance, it makes the traditional tools of investing and valuation inadequate. Pre-Revenue is the domain of venture capitalists, whose model can support more failures. In Peter Theil's book *Zero to One*, he explains that a venture capital fund will invest in 20 such companies with the expectation that maybe 1 or 2 will succeed while 18–19 will fail (failing is…worth $0, shutter, or go bankrupt). The 1 or 2 that succeed will be dramatically successful, more than covering the losses from the other companies in the fund. Think about the Facebook and Googles of the world covering the losses of numerous unnamed and forgotten startups. That's an investment model that is hard to stomach for a retail investor.

As such, the desired characteristics in the IPO Tool Kit I provided cannot adequately analyze companies that are pre-revenue or not generating any sales yet. It's beyond my personal skill set, experience, and risk tolerance. Simply put, I want to see a company generate revenue and grow that revenue. I'm okay if they aren't profitable yet, but I need to know they have a product and can sell it. I don't want to guess (and pray) that it will generate revenue in the near or distant future.

CHAPTER 22

Brand Equity

One of the best qualities a company can have is brand equity. With strong brand equity, customers come back regularly to buy a product or service because they love it and gain so much value from it. It can also mean they love it so much that they buy it for their friends, parents, kids, and other loved ones and preach to others about how great it is, providing free marketing for the brand. Brand equity is something you "know when you see it" but there are also three empirical metrics that can hint at strong brand equity: high gross profit margins, global awareness, and repeat purchases.

But first, so let's give brand equity a formal definition:

> *"Brand equity describes the level of sway a brand name has in the minds of consumers, and the value of having a brand that is identifiable and well thought of. Organizations establish brand equity by creating positive experiences that entice consumers to continue purchasing from them over competitors who make similar products."*

Source: www.marketingevolution.com

High Gross Margins

What do Nike Air Jordan shoes, Ferrari racecars, lululemon yoga pants, and Louis Vuitton handbags have in common? Incredibly high gross profit margins. Gross profit is how much profit remains after subtracting all of the direct inputs that are needed to make it. For an additional pair of Nike shoes, we're just counting the leather, plastic, glue, box, and labor that assembles it all. For a Louis Vuitton bag, the cost of goods sold would include leather, paint, glue, and labor used to hand assemble the bag. For a Ferrari, it's the engine, wheels, leather seats, paint, and all the labor to assemble the car. For lululemon yoga pants, it's the specialty fabric and labor to cut and sew it, as well as the delivery cost to get it to retail stores.

Exhibit 32 – Cost of Goods Sold (COGS) Per Dollar of Revenue

Image: Graphic Design by Tram Nguyen
Source: Nike, Ferrari, Lululemon, and Louis Vuitton Moet Hennessy 10-K filings.

Here's the math:

Cost of Goods Sold (COGS) includes the cost of materials, labor, and any other inputs directly used for manufacturing a product or delivering a service.

Gross Profit   = Revenue - Cost of Goods Sold (COGS)

Gross Margins = Gross Profit / Revenue

But popular luxury products like Louis Vuitton bags and Lululemon yoga pants cost a lot and don't cost that much to make relative to their retail prices. What gives? Why do people pay so much for something that costs less to actually produce? Where are the competitors flooding in to develop a similar product with lower prices? What about all of those perfect competition graphs I drew in my economics class showing profits go to zero?

The answer is brand equity.

There isn't a single data source that will tell you a company has strong brand equity. It will require reading several sections of the S-1 and external sources to understand how customers interact with the company. The Prospectus Summary and Business sections are a good start, while the Selected Consolidated Financial and Other Data will provide gross and profit margin figures.

That is the power and value of brand equity. Brand equity is built over decades of producing high quality products, strong marketing to engrain the brand, its logo, its mission and message into the minds of the customer and to ultimately teach the customer what to associate with the brand. Brand equity is built on the continued delivery of amazing products (experience) while consistent marketing keeps the brand top of mind (awareness).

Fancy Handbags

For Louis Vuitton (LV) bags, the unique design, excellent quality, and global recognition of elegance is an aspirational item for women and men around the world. The bags are expensive and associate the carrier with luxury, good taste, elegance, and wealth. This brand equity is built with both classic and innovative designs such as the timeless shape of the Speedy or Neverfull bag with its globally recognized LV logo and a price tag of over $3,000. They frequently have hip and modern design collaborations with streetwear brands like Supreme to appeal to a younger audience. Strong messaging of luxury grace billboards and magazines while the brand buys back unsold inventory to destroy so it can prevent LV products from ever going on sale, which would dilute the prestige of the brand. The world's most famous stars contribute to marketing campaigns for LV to reemphasize the message of timeless elegance. Year after year, customers save up and come back for re-peat purchases because they love the functional use of the product and how it makes them feel: exclusive and special.

Louis Vuitton Moet Hennessy was formed in 1987 under the merger of fashion house Louis Vuitton (founded in 1854) with Moët Hennessy, a company formed after the 1971 merger between the champagne producer Moët & Chandon and cognac producer Hennessy. LVMH, the French lux-ury conglomerate, sells everything from the LV logo embossed leather bags, famous Moet & Chandon champagne, and Hennessy cognac, fancy Hublot watches, Tiffany jewelry, a myriad of makeup brands, and designer brands like Christian Dior across its seven operating segments (called "houses"), which are an umbrella for several luxury brands. This luxury conglomerate exemplifies brand equity. Their handbags, champagne, makeup stores, and watches are well-known brands throughout the world. Their luxury prod-ucts appeal to a growing middle class throughout the world who aspire to achieve and live the luxurious life reflected in their advertising, store expe-riences, and commercials. Their premium quality products stand the test of time and they are able to profit from very high gross margins as a result of the allure and prestige of their luxury brands.

Fancy Yoga Pants

With Lululemon, the brand communicates a healthy, active, and progressive lifestyle centered around fitness, self-awareness, and spirituality. No doubt other competitors can make yoga pants, but these pants put you into a com-munity. For Lululemon, brand equity is built from both their yoga pants and the in-store yoga classes. Yes, they had the see-through pants manufacturing issue in 2014, but they apologized and fixed the issue for their customers. They are often credited with starting the athleisure movement in the U.S. as their early adopters—women who took yoga classes—continued on their day without changing out of the stylish and functional yoga pants. They build and nurture loyalty through their community of yoga practitioners in their stores, which double as a yoga studio and retail space. This sense of community encourages a healthy and fit lifestyle and repeat purchases. Health and fitness are secular trends that Lululemon taps into with their quality products.

LVMUY, the ticker for Louis Vuitton's American Depository Rights (ADR) stock in the U.S. was first available on December 24, 2002. Buying $1,000 of LVMUY stock on the first day would lead to a total return of 1,923%, or annual returns of 18%, turning that initial $1,000 investment into $20,229 as of December 31, 2020.

Buying $1,000 of Lululemon Athletica (LULU) stock on the day of its IPO, July 27, 2007, would lead to a cumulative return of 2,386%, or an annualized return of 27%, turning that initial $1,000 investment into $24,859 as of December 31, 2020.

Thought exercise: What is another brand that is admired and loved? A good starting point is thinking about a brand that both you and your parents love and one that you might pass on to your kids. Those are multi-generational brands that have powerful brand equity.

PART 3

SHOULD I INVEST?

CHAPTER 23

When Do You Hold Forever?

If I were to apply the Tool Kit and analyze the characteristics of the major companies mentioned in the book, this is the table I would get. A check indicates that the company has the characteristic desirable for a long-term investment.

Exhibit 33 - Check List Summary

IPO Check List	Netflix	Apple	Google	Facebook	LVMH	McDonald's	Proctor & Gamble	Nike	Amazon	Tesla
Innovative Products	✓					✓			✓	✓
Dominant Market Share	✓		✓	✓		✓	✓	✓		
New Category/Solve a Problem		✓		✓			✓			✓
Big Profits		✓	✓	✓	✓	✓				
Large Total Addressable Market (TAM)	✓	✓	✓	✓			✓		✓	✓
Essential			✓			✓	✓		✓	
Global Reach		✓	✓	✓	✓	✓		✓		✓
Secular Trend	✓	✓	✓					✓	✓	✓
Corporate Culture	✓	✓		✓			✓		✓	
Brand Equity and Customer Loyalty		✓		✓	✓	✓	✓	✓	✓	✓

Let's revisit our assumption that we have $1,000 and we want to find an excellent company to invest in early on and hold it "forever". Forever is not necessarily forever, but more of a placeholder for expressing our long-term perspective. You want to hold the stock until you need money for things that come along in life such as paying for a wedding or a house. When you have the mindset that you will hold the stock "forever," you remove the stress and energy that comes with monitoring the stock every single day and reading any and every news article, opinion piece, or Wall Street sell-side analyst commentary.

While these activities can be fun at first, it is simply time consuming and over time adds little incremental value to your understanding of the company. Processing all of that data, or noise would be too much work for an average retail investor. Instead, we want a company to meet a very high threshold to satisfy the initial requirements of being a "hold forever stock" so we don't have to worry and can go on with our busy lives, trusting the analysis we did at the beginning is sufficient. I want to stress Warren Buffett's adage of "time in the market, not timing the market".

Art, Not Science

I will be the first to admit that investing in IPOs is more of an art than a science. So much is out of your control, such as how the market receives new products and services, how the company is actually run, and whether new entrants come and reduce your company to smithereens or it's the other way around and your company successfully combats new entrants. Any IPO investment you consider should have a majority of the Tool Kit's characteristics checked off and firmly in its favor. It'll be impossible to have it all, as no company can forever be immune to competition, evolving consumer taste, nor address the needs of every new secular trend.

With regards to meeting the criteria of the IPO Tool Kit, the more characteristics a company exhibits, the better. Even if it has just a few, it could be a successful company because so much remains to be seen in the future, which is unpredictable. Ultimately, it will require you to understand the full picture of the company and ask yourself, can I hold this forever and not be worried about it at night? My approach is to check off at least seven of the

Tool Kit requirements to ensure the company has the necessary attributes to grow, compete, and be a market share leader.

Have Faith

After all of the analysis, running through the S-1 prospectus, reading as much as you can, watching the roadshow video on www.RetailRoadshow.com, and checking off the characteristics on the Tool Kit, you now have a better understanding of the company.

You will ultimately have to make a call: invest or pass.

Simply put, you just have to trust that your analysis is correct and have faith in your analysis, the company, and its prospects. The onus of finding companies that meet the Tool Kit's characteristics creates a very high threshold, but that just means we are insured if one of our criteria is wrong that the others might be right and contribute to the company's success. Over time, you'll realize the more you invest and learn, the more your intuition will be correct. As you invest and gain analysis experience, that gut call will be that much more effective and directionally correct. After the careful research is completed, I ultimately want to walk away believing in the company's story. Their vision to change the world, provide an amazing product, revolutionize the way you consume a product or service—whatever it is, you should be able to believe in it as a winning story because your research provided the proof.

"Forever" is just a very long holding period

To echo the "forever" themes written about in the book, you need to be comfortable with a long-term hold period. Realize that the company's lofty goals or the investments they put into R&D take time to come to fruition. Let the company grow, make mistakes, and evolve. Do not react to the immediate or short-term price gains or losses. The price history of the stock will not be a straight line up, but jagged and volatile over long periods of time. The shorter the time frame, the more volatile the stock will seem to be. Zooming out for a view that is over years and decades instead of days, the price chart will look much smoother. There will undoubtedly be bumps along the way, but in the long term the company's success in executing and delivering will be translated into stock gains. If I had to scribble it on a napkin, it would look something like this:

Exhibit 34 – Days, Years, & Decades

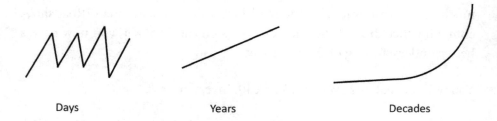

Days   Years   Decades

No matter what method the company chooses to go public, either traditional IPO, SPAC, or direct listing, or if it was spun off from a larger parent company, it will require the same amount of research and analysis to determine if it is worth investing in. The methods used to analyze these companies at the IPO can be applied to any company days, months, and years after they start publicly trading.

CHAPTER 24

Is this IPO going to the moon🚀?

Scene:

It's 5:30 pm on a sunny summer evening. We're joining Albert "Auto-Index", Raymond "Retail Investor", and Allen "Active" at Pez Cantina in downtown Los Angeles. Happy hour just started and Raymond gathers his investment group chat buddies for a drink to catch up. Traffic is always bad in Los Angeles, but the Lakers have a finals home game tonight, so it was a good opportunity to rally the troops and wait out the traffic.

Waiter: Gentlemen, my name is Jose and I'll be your server today. What I can get you?

Raymond: I'll have a glass of red wine, thank you.

Allen: Whiskey sour for me, please.

Albert: It's been a long day, so I'll have a margarita with double tequila to take the edge off. Thank you.

Jose: Excellent, I'll be right back with your drinks.

Raymond: How are you guys doing? Thanks for coming out. You guys were blowing up my text messages today. "Are you buying the Unicorn IPO?"

Another reads, "Is this IPO going to the moon 🚀?" I couldn't get any work done due to the constant buzzing of the notifications so I had to put the phone on mute.

Allen: It's nuts. My coworker asked me if she should sell her dogecoins to buy Unicorn shares.

Man...this is a hot IPO. I've seen the cars around LA, there is a long waitlist apparently.

Albert: What the heck are dogecoins? Yeah, the waitlist is a few months out. Or maybe even longer, they are still dealing with the semiconductor chip shortage so they don't even have the parts to make these cars.

Raymond: I know the Unicorn S-1 has been out for a while and the CEO Tram was just on CNBC with Jim Cramer. She sat shotgun and let him drive the new model around—he seemed to really like it. He came out and supported the stock on his show.

Allen: I was able to start reading the S-1 a few weeks ago. I loved what I saw, it checks all the boxes. I'm bullish on the company. Innovative cars, rabid fan base, recurring business model because they sell apps and fully autonomous driving software. Not to mention it is beloved in the U.S., Europe, and China. They'll launch the robotaxi network soon too, so your car can be a taxi while you work and make money for you. The car will literally pay for itself. LITERALLY.

Raymond: Wow. I don't know how I feel about other people sitting in my car while I'm not there, but I can't argue against it making trips to pay for the monthly payment. That's genius. Albert, I know you are the index fund guy...so it was shocking to see you blow up my text today. Are you really thinking about buying shares of Unicorn?

Jose: Gentlemen, here are your drinks. Sorry, I couldn't help but overhear your conversation. I'm definitely buying some shares of Unicorn; you'd be a fool not to.

Albert: Thank you Jose. Sorry to rain on the parade but I follow the words of Jack Bogle and Warren Buffett; the S&P 500 index is where I want to be invested. I love the fact that I can diversify and get all the top companies easily and add to my position every month. It doesn't matter if it's SPY, VOO, or VTI; in the end these ETFs capture the dynamism of the greatest companies in the U.S. To me, it's a no-hassle strategy that beats a lot of active mutual fund managers and hedge funds over the long term. The ability to set it on a monthly automatic investing schedule is great because I don't have time to do the deep research on Unicorn or the next hot IPO.

Allen: I like and enjoy researching stocks, personally. To me, it's thrilling and being able to say I invested in a small company early on and earn amazing gains is a major flex. The research and debates are fun, I like the thrill of the volatility and the risk involved. It's gonna be a wild ride with this IPO. Even my non-finance friends are texting me about it.

Jose: I'm liking everything I read and hear from the CEO. Tram seems to have lots of new models in the works and international markets to expand into. They have a large total addressable market because, in theory, anyone driving a gasoline powered car is a potential customer.

Allen: Yes! My man, I'm with you. Unicorn has the best tech and it's on the cutting edge of every trend. It will be a household name if only they can build their cars fast enough.

Raymond: I just got a text from my dad asking me about it. He wants me to buy 100 shares for him. Look—without a doubt, the thrill of finding the next Netflix or Tesla or Amazon is an amazing high but it's hard and the fact is, we'll end up with a few duds as well. Even with the great hedge funds and mutual funds, few actually beat the market over the long term. The ones that do beat the market are heralded as geniuses and the media shines the bright lights on them, but they are the few exceptions. The majority of active fund managers underperform the benchmark. Everyone talks about Lynch, Ackman, Dalio, Buffet, Cathie Wood, etc. but no one talks about how rare it is to reach that pinnacle of excellence.

Jose: I'm a big fan of the WallStreetBets Reddit and I love reading about stocks. I try to follow as much as can, given my busy schedule. There isn't enough time in the day to learn about all of these companies even if it were my full-time job.

Albert: That's why I like the passive route. I really believe putting your money into a large and diversified index fund is the best route for most people. It's easy, it's cheap because the expense ratio is very low, and it works. You don't beat the market, but you don't trail it either. And guess what, the market goes up over time. You get to hitch a ride on that gravy train.

Allen: If you're okay with being average, then that works. But I crave the thrill of beating the market and sharing the ideas with everyone.

Raymond: Most retail investors will have the majority of their investments in something that is automatic and passive, like a monthly contribution to a retirement 401-K or IRA or squirreling away a fixed amount each month and put it into an index fund or mutual fund. Look, I got kids and a full-time job. I have salsa dance lessons and a honey-do list of stuff around the house that needs to be fixed. I love the investment group chat, but I don't have time to read into the 400-page S-1s or analyze every page of the SPAC presentations for every new stock that comes around.

Albert: I think the truth is, for most people, the passive strategy is the winner. It's a winner because we all think we can beat the market; we all think we are the exception to the rule. But we can't--the data proves that. People forget about the failures of funds like Long-Term Capital Management, Tiger Funds, SAC Capital, Melvin Capital, Archegos and numerous other hedge funds and mutual funds that have closed up over the years.

Allen: But sometimes, you get that itch. You see a headline and you know that company is the next big thing. Maybe you use it all the time or your kids love it, and you know it's a great investment. People definitely do not want to miss out on the next big thing, even though they will eventually own it in an index fund if it does consistently well. FOMO, the fear of missing out, is for real.

Jose: I've been hearing about Unicorn from a lot of different people and definitely have the itch to just buy some shares. I always have a case of FOMO and don't want to miss out on this hot IPO but also realistically will not sit down with the 400-page S-1 to read cover to cover. Is there a cliff notes version somewhere?

Raymond: Look, there is a middle ground. You don't have to dedicate every single free moment to studying the next hot stock. I personally do a hybrid approach. My 401-K is in an index fund and my wife's 401-K is in a target date fund. Diversified and steady. I have a taxable account where I invest my spare cash and use that to buy great companies. I got a few dogecoins on my Coinbase account because those damn Instagram memes you guys share got to me. I follow the IPOs and in the rare instance that I feel a company might have the 13 characteristics mentioned in Nam Nguyen's book, I'll do the research and decide whether to invest. I would say the majority of my assets are in index funds, but I do get the itch to buy some stocks and love to read into them when I feel compelled enough to invest directly in the stock. If I do end up buying the stock, whether on the first day of its IPO or later on, I plan on holding it as a long-term investment. I prefer to know as much about the company as I can before I commit and not just go off someone's recommendation.

Allen: I agree, everyone is different. Everyone has different risk tolerance and goals ahead of them. With stocks and IPOs, there is lots of volatility. The big up days are great; you gain 20% and feel like a genius. The large down days hurt like hell; you are down 30% and panic sets in. You blow up everyone's messages to see if your friends are selling. You debate whether you should buy more or cut your losses here. For someone who doesn't follow the stock closely, the volatility will be a roller coaster and create a lot of stress.

Albert: You'll win some and lose some, and on average—you will be average. But you can be average without expending all of that energy by getting an index fund. Remember, the average is a positive return. You're gonna grow your wealth, just at a slower pace. But it can be at an even slower pace, if you are indeed bad at stock picking. I mean, I held onto Netflix for the first 5 years since it went public and it was just dead flat. Not until they started the streaming service did it have its amazing run. And now, looking back with 20/20 hindsight...I wonder why I didn't plow all of my money into Netflix and retire early. *Sigh*. c'est la vie.

Jose: Five years? Wow, that's a long time. I'm a day trader at heart, I love buying and selling for a quick profit. It's a little like gambling, but my technical analysis has given me an edge.

Raymond: Sure, I'll admit, I love reading about and buying the latest IPO—especially if it's a brand or service I use all the time. I don't do it all the time, nor do I do it with all of my money, but it provides a nice addition to my core portfolio holdings of index funds. I sleep better at night with research and due diligence done on a company. If things go well, great. If they don't, I can always come back and decide to hold or dissect what went wrong and perhaps decide to sell. I love putting in the work, but am just more selective with which IPO or SPAC or direct listing deserves that time commitment.

Jose: I think we can all agree that going with TRILL as their ticker is just a brilliant move for Unicorn. They aren't a meme stock but they are tapping into the younger demographic as their target market, for the cars and the shares. We'll see what the first day of trading is like, I am guessing there is gonna be a big pop and shares will be up 50-100%. The CNBC and Bloomberg people have been talking and hyping it non-stop.

Albert: There is going to be massive demand and massive volatility.

Allen: Picking stocks is not for the faint of heart. Everyone is a genius in a bull market when things are going up every day, but in a bear market is where you'll find the true investors. A lot of people can't stand to see their returns turn red and lose money, on paper. They'll pull out and cut their losses. If you buy IPOs, you'll need "diamond hands"—steady discipline to hold onto the stocks through the rough times where it might be beaten down. Lots of people say they want a stock to crash so they can buy it for cheap, but when that moment arises very few people follow through. Fear takes over. You always ask yourself: can it go lower?

Albert: Outside of someone in the finance industry, rarely will a portfolio be managed by one person doing all the stock research. In fact, professionals usually have teams of portfolio managers and research analysts managing a portfolio of 50-100 stocks. For an individual to do it and do it well, over long periods of time? That's a statistical anomaly.

Raymond: You'll have to pick a few stocks and do some research to find out if it's for you. You'll have some wins and losses, and lessons learned from those. The more you do it, the better you become. As your life enters different stages, you'll find you have different interests, risks, and things you want to save up for. Those will all directly impact and adjust how you invest and think about stocks.

Jose: Allen, since you looked at it, what your feelings on Unicorn?

Allen: Yup, did the due diligence on the S-1 and tried to track down the characteristics on the tool kit. After a couple of IPOs, you know where to go and what to look for. No way anyone reads 400+ pages so don't worry Jose. I'm sure not a single investment banker reads it cover to cover. Here are my thoughts. I like the company and the way it's being run. The management team is investing for the long term and is doing a traditional IPO to raise a boatload of cash to build out more factories around the world. They are having a hard time meeting demand. Seems smart to ditch the SPAC and direct listing routes for a regular IPO because they wanted to raise $25 bn in capital. Valuation wise, they look to be expensive with a P/E ratio of 100x but they have a decent PEG of 2.4 due to 40% growth rate. They have earnings potential from that robotaxi network that I mentioned but they can also start charging for their now free nationwide charging station network as well, which will boost profits. When people stop in the stations to charge their car, they load up on bottled drinks and snacks at the convenience stores too. They sell water and soda for a 100% mark up so that's a boost to profit margins. Look, electric vehicles are a huge secular trend. The TAM is huge and the cars' look and logo are well known around the world.

Raymond: Did you see any potential risks?

Allen: Obviously the competition, the global auto giants that are backed by their nation's government. Cars employ a lot of people in the supply chain, from the manufacturing, to the repair and servicing, to the development of in-car apps. Germany, Japan, Korea, and China aren't going to sit idle and let Unicorn dominate the market. Cars depend on batteries and chips, which are both in short supply these days. Cars compete with phones and computers for the same parts, which can drive up the COGS on each car and reduce profits. They also depend on rare earth minerals that are mined in China, where we currently face some economic and political tensions. Competition is the key risk, but the TAM is big enough to support multiple car brands just like it is now with gas powered cars.

Jose: Great analysis Allen, thanks for sharing.

Albert: Looks like we're done with our drinks and it's halftime. The Lakers are up 7 over the Nets. Probably a good time to hit the road. Anyone wanna grab an LA street dog with me? After my workout, it'll hold me down until I get home. The vendor is right outside and the bacon, bell pepper, and onion smell is irresistible.

Raymond: Yup, I'm in for a dog. I enjoyed the drinks and conversation. It was great hearing everyone's different perspectives. I gotta spend some time researching the stock and digging into all aspects of its business model and potential risks. Look – we need to zone out the media hype. It might indeed go to the moon, but I want to know why. Allen, let's compare notes as I am sure we'll have more than a few data points in common. If I buy, I plan on holding it for the long term. You know what they say, "measure twice and cut once."

Jose: No pain, no gain, right?

Allen: I'll leave y'all with some words of wisdom: Most of the activity in the stock market is buying and selling stocks. Most of the gains in the market are made by holding stocks.

CHAPTER 25

Conclusion

I hope you are empowered to confidently invest as a result of being more knowledgeable about the IPO process and better equipped to analyze a company with my IPO Tool Kit as a guide. As you research more companies, the tool kit will evolve to fit your style and perspective on what you think makes a company worthy of being held "forever" or for a long time. Akin to a recipe passed down through multiple generations, everyone will modify the portions and ingredients to adjust it to their tastebuds. You might find that my Tool Kit overemphasizes a characteristic or is missing one altogether. In which case, you are free and encouraged to modify it for your own research needs going forward.

Analyzing an IPO is a very time consuming and difficult thing to do, as it requires an intense amount of focus and energy. The payoff is also uncertain. You aren't always going to get it right, and what you thought was a great company can disappoint while a weaker company could resolve its issues and become an iconic global firm. It takes time to learn about a company and its place in an industry. There will be mistakes and unknown variables, so those can prove to be valuable lessons going forward. You'll get better the more you do it, just like with anything in life.

Don't rush it. The IPO window is usually a few weeks from S-1 filing to the first day of trading. You don't have to invest in the company on the first trading day. It is better to use your time researching and working through the checklist to build confidence and conviction. Sometimes, you can spend a lot of time on research to come away thinking it's not a great company. Don't consider this time wasted; consider it time invested in sharpening your stock analysis skills for the next IPO, and the one after that.

So, if you aren't missing out by not investing on the very first day of public trading, then it must be true that the IPO Tool Kit can be applied to researching a company on any day after its IPO. This tool kit can be used to analyze any company at any point in time and is really a broader tool for identifying great companies, no matter if the IPO is next week or occurred 25 years ago. Better a little late, but with clear conviction, than to rush into an uncertain investment on the first day a company goes public.

BIBLIOGRAPHY

Chapter 2: Initial Public Offering (IPO)

Smith, Tim (2020). "Greenshoe Option". Investopedia. Online. Available at: https://www.investopedia.com/terms/g/greenshoe.asp. Updated: 11/11/2020

Golub, Jonathan (2021). "2020: Year in Review." U.S. Equity Strategy Navigator. Data retrieved from Factset.

Chapter 3: Special Purpose Acquisition Company (SPAC)

SPACinsider (2020). "SPAC IPO insurances since 2013." SPACinsider. Online. Available at: https://spacinsider.com/stats/.

Klausner, Michael, Michael Ohlrogge and Emily Ruan (2020). "A Sober Look at SPACs". Yale Journal on Regulation, Stanford Law and Economics Olin Working Paper No. 559, NYU Law and Economics Research Paper No. 20-48. Available online at: https://papers.ssrn.com/sol3/papers.cfm?abstract_id=3720919
Updated: 3/6/2021

Laughlin, Lauren Silva (2020). "Breakingviews - SPACs give Wall Street another slice of the pie". Reuters. Online. Available at: https://www.reuters.com/article/us-usa-spac-breakingviews/breakingviews-spacs-give-wall-street-another-slice-of-the-pie-idUSKBN27J24L

Bryant, Chris (2021). "SPACs Get Smacked Down by a More Assertive SEC". Bloomberg. Online.

Available at: https://www.bloomberg.com/opinion/articles/2021-04-13/the-sec-s-spac-crackdown-may-have-a-chilling-effect

Chapter 4: Direct Listing

Lee, Allison Herren and Caroline A. Crenshaw (2020). "Statement on Primary Direct Listings". Securities and Exchange Commission (SEC). Online. Available at: https://www.sec.gov/news/public-statement/lee-crenshaw-listings-2020-12-23
Updated: 12/23/2020

Thorne, James (2021). "Roblox Valued at $45.3B in Record Setting Direct Listing". Pitchbook. Online. Available at: https://pitchbook.com/news/articles/roblox-gaming-direct-listing-valuation

Root, Al (2019). "DowDuPont Is Splitting Into 3 Companies. Here's Everything You Need to Know". Barron's. Online. Available at: https://www.barrons.com/articles/dowdupont-spinoff-dow-dupont-corteva-51556552428

Lin, Jinghong. (2020). "Can Direct Listings Disrupt the IPO Process?". McGill Business Review. Online. Available at: https://mcgillbusinessreview.com/articles/can-direct-listing-disrupt-the-ipo-process

Chapter 6: A Unicorn Goes Public

Gurley, Bill. (August 2020). "Going Public Circa 2020; Door #3: The SPAC". Above the Crowd blog. Online. Available at: https://abovethecrowd.com/2020/08/23/going-public-circa-2020-door-3-the-spac/

Chapter 8: Navigating the S-1 Prospectus

Albertsons Companies. (July 18, 2020). Form S-1, Initial Registration Form. Available at: https://sec.report/Document/0001193125-20-172409/

Facebook. (February 1, 2012) Form S-1, Initial Registration Form. Available at: https://www.sec.gov/Archives/edgar/data/1326801/000119312512034517/d287954ds1.htm

Unity Software. (August 24, 2020) Form S-1, Initial Registration Form. Available at: https://www.sec.gov/Archives/edgar/data/1810806/000119312520227862/d908875ds1.htm#toc908875_1

AirBnB. (November 16, 2020). Form S-1, Initial Registration Form. Available at: https://www.sec.gov/Archives/edgar/data/1559720/000119312520294801/d81668ds1.htm

Hilton Worldwide Companies Inc. (September 12, 2013). Form S-1, Initial Registration Form. Available at: https://www.sec.gov/Archives/edgar/data/1585689/000119312513364703/d593452ds1.htm

Coinbase Global Inc. (February 25, 2021). Form S-1, Initial Registration Form. Available at: https://www.sec.gov/Archives/edgar/data/1679788/000162828021003168/coinbaseglobalincs-1.htm

Roku, Inc. (September 1, 2017) Form S-1, Initial Registration Form. Available at: https://www.sec.gov/Archives/edgar/data/1428439/000119312517275689/d403225ds1.htm

Chapter 10: Innovative Products

Netflix Corporation. (May 22, 2002). Form S-1, Initial Registration Form. Available at: https://www.sec.gov/Archives/edgar/data/1065280/000101287002002475/d424b4.htm.

Richtel, Matt (2008). "Cable Prices Keep Rising, and Customers Keep Paying". New York Times. Online. Available at: https://www.nytimes.com/2008/05/24/technology/24cable.html

Olenski, Steve (2017). "Why Content Will Always Be King", Forbes, June 21. Online. Available at: https://www.forbes.com/sites/steveolenski/2017/06/21/why-content-will-always-always-king/?sh=6b4cc328eb37

Chapter 12: Win A New Category/Solve a Problem

Enberg, Jasmine (2019). "Global Digital Ad Spending 2019", eMarketer. Online. Available at: https://www.emarketer.com/content/global-digital-ad-spending-2019
Updated: 3/28/2019

Smith, Brad (2015). "Intuit's CEO on building a Design-Driven Company". Harvard Business Review. Online. Available at: https://hbr.org/2015/01/intuits-ceo-on-building-a-design-driven-company

Thiel, Peter and Blake Masters (2014). "Zero to One: Notes on Startups, or How to Build the Future". Crown Business Publishing. ISBN: 978-0804139298

Chapter 17: Secular Trends

Callinan, James L. (2020). "Catching the Wave: Why Secular Growth Matters ". www.Osterweis.com. Online. Available at: https://www.osterweis.com/insights/cyclical_vs_secular

Twin, Alexandra (2021). "Secular". Investopedia. Online. Available at: https://www.investopedia.com/terms/s/secular.asp

Mellow, Craig (2021). "It's Not Just Coupang: E-Commerce Upstarts Are Flourishing Everywhere ". Barron's. Online. Available at: https://www.barrons.com/articles/its-not-just-coupang-e-commerce-upstarts-are-flourishing-everywhere-51615552200

Cramer-Flood, Ethan (2021). "Global Ecommerce Update 2021". eMarketer. Online. Available at: https://www.emarketer.com/content/global-ecommerce-update-2021

Chapter 18: Risks

AirBnB. (November 16, 2020). Form S-1, Initial Registration Form. Available at: https://www.sec.gov/Archives/edgar/data/1559720/000119312520294801/d81668ds1.htm

The We Company. (August 14, 2019). Form S-1, Initial Registration Form. Available at: https://www.sec.gov/Archives/edgar/data/1533523/00011931251 9220499/d781982ds1.htm

Alibaba Group Holding Limited. (May 6, 2014). Form F-1 Registration Statement. Available at: https://www.sec.gov/Archives/edgar/data/1577552/ 000119312514184994/d709111df1.htm

Chapter 21: SPAC Valuation

Churchill Capital Corporation IV. (March 2021). "Form S-4". SEC.com. Available at: https://sec.report/Document/0001104659-21-039318/

Lucid Motors. (February 2021). "Lucid Investor Presentation". Available at: https://lucid-ir.s3-us-west-2.amazonaws.com/lucid-investor-presentatio n-february-2021.pdf

Tse, Crystal, Edward Ludlow, and Dinesh Nair. (2021). "Lucid Motors Is Said to Near Deal to List Via Klein's SPAC". Bloomberg. Online. Available at: https://www.bloomberg.com/news/articles/2021-02-20/lucid-motors-is-sai d-to-near-deal-to-go-public-via-klein-s-spac

Clinton, Doug and Gene Munster (2021). "SPACs are Venture Capital in Public Markets". Loup Ventures. Online. Available at: https://loupventures. com/spacs-are-venture-capital-in-public-markets

Thiel, Peter and Blake Masters (2014). "Zero to One: Notes on Startups, or How to Build the Future". Crown Business Publishing. ISBN: 978-0804139298

Chapter 22: Brand Equity

Marketing Evolution (2021). "What is Brand Equity? How to Build and Measure It". Marketing Evolution. Online. Available at: https://www.mar-ketingevolution.com/marketing-essentials/what-is-brand-equity-marketin g-evolution

ABOUT THE AUTHOR

Nam Viet Nguyen has worked as an equity research analyst covering IPOs, SPACs, and direct listings for over a decade. He's passionate about financial literacy and lectures middle school students through undergraduates on investing in stocks. He lives and works in Texas with his wife and son.

For more information visit www.namvietnguyen.com

CPSIA information can be obtained
at www.ICGtesting.com
Printed in the USA
LVHW080516290721
693947LV00018B/996/J